Duibltime ...

DUE	DATE DUE

STRAYA

Rhododendrons
and
Azaleas

Rhododendrons and Azaleas

I. F. La Croix

With line illustrations by the author

David & Charles : Newton Abbot

0 7153 5944 4

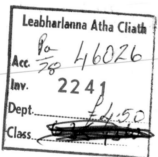
Set in 11 on 13pt Baskerville
and printed in Great Britain by
Butler & Tanner Ltd, Frome and London
for David & Charles (Holdings) Limited
South Devon House Newton Abbot Devon

Contents

List of Illustrations

PLATES

7

LINE DRAWINGS

Introduction

Gardening books and articles proliferate, and anyone who is planning to add to their number is bound to ask himself if he has anything new to contribute. I think that there is a great deal still to be said about rhododendrons and azaleas. No group of plants infects its devotees with greater enthusiasm, but there is a great gulf between the specialist and the 'average gardener' (if such an animal exists), who thinks of rhododendrons in terms of the naturalized *R. ponticum* that forms dense thickets in so many woods and estates, and the 'hardy hybrids' which, with perhaps a few hybrid azaleas, are the sole representatives of the genus in so many small and medium-sized gardens.

I am sure that anyone who grows even a moderately representative selection must be familiar with remarks such as 'I didn't know you got rhododendrons as small as that' when a visitor is shown something like *R. radicans*, or even 'but I thought all rhododendrons were mauve'.

No plants are more worth a place in even a small garden, and few are less trouble to maintain in good health. They do not need regular spraying and pruning, and given a good start, should delight the gardener for the rest of his life with the minimum of attention. Most rhododendrons are evergreen and thus give value throughout the year, not only when in flower. There is great variety of colour, size and shape of foliage. This is where the older hybrids fall short, as they are almost all undistinguished and indistinguishable in form and foliage, but there are many good modern hybrids, in any case more suitable in size for most present-day gardens, that are much better all round plants. There are also many species which are in every way good garden plants. These easy going species and attractive hybrids are not too difficult to obtain although you may not be able to find them in the nearest garden centre. At the end of the book there is a list of nurseries which stock a good selection of rhododendrons and I have no doubt there are more that I do not know. Most of these will send plants if none are conveniently near.

Having emphasized the fact that rhododendrons are possibly the ideal plants for a modern, labour-saving garden, it is necessary to admit that, as most people know, they are not suitable for gardens on chalk or lime. There are preparations which are supposed to help, but I think that on a really alkaline soil one must forget about rhododendrons and console oneself with plants such as roses, cherries and clematis. Certainly small growing types can be grown in tubs and raised peat beds—this is dealt with in the appropriate chapter.

The descriptions of species and hybrids are gathered together towards the end of the book, in the belief that this makes the text more readable than if these descriptions were scattered through it. Such descriptions can be approached in one of two ways. They can be of sufficient botanical detail that an unknown species can be identified by reference to them, or they can give an indication of what sort of plant the grower could expect were he to purchase one. As this book is aimed at the person who is not already a specialist, but rather a potential convert, I have chosen the second approach. Those who want botanical details will be able to find them in *The Rhododendron Handbook Part I*, published by the Royal Horticultural Society, and in *The Species of Rhododendron*, published by the Rhododendron Society, which although out of date in some ways, is still invaluable, particularly when used in conjunction with the Handbook.

CHAPTER 1

Classification and Distribution

It is possible to cultivate a garden for years in happy ignorance of even the names of most of its inhabitants. I have known a few people like this, and some of them have been what is called green-fingered, so that any broken branch stuck in the ground sprouted, and any seedling pulled up by the roots and roughly replanted, flourished. But most of us prefer to follow the accepted rules if we can, and like to have some idea of the names, origins and relationships of the plants we grow.

The genus *Rhododendron* belongs to one of the two dozen great families of flowering plants, the Ericaceae. With the genus *Erica* (the heaths) it dominates the family, but the latter also contains quite a number of smaller genera of horticultural importance, such as *Pieris, Kalmia, Gaultheria* and *Calluna*. Almost all share a preference for acid soils with plenty of humus, moist yet well drained.

Rhododendron is a very successful genus, with something over 900 species at the last count. It seems to be still in the course of evolution, as many species are very variable. Many of the more widespread species have a number of geographical forms—often when first discovered, these were described as separate species, but when intermediate forms were subsequently discovered, it became apparent that the whole complex was in fact one variable species. Presumably if, in the course of many thousands of years, changes of climate and physical relief occurred and the intervening forms were wiped out, the plants at the extremes of the range would develop into distinct species. Possibly too, some of the variation is the result of hybridization having taken place at some time in the past.

A species, after all, is a man-made concept, or at least man's interpretation of Nature. It is convenient to classify plants, in the same way as a philatelist will have his collection arranged rather than all jumbled up. With plants, too, there is more than one method of arrangement. The classification of rhododendrons is based on consideration of characters such as the habit of the plant; its leaf-shape; the presence or absence of scales; the occurrence of hairs; the presence and appearance of glands; the number of parts in the calyx and corolla and the shape and colour of the latter in particular; the number and position of the stamens and the shape and appearance of the ovary and fruit.

Azalea was originally described as a separate genus, differing from *Rhododendron* in having 5 stamens instead of 10 or more, and having deciduous instead of evergreen leaves. At that time, evergreen azaleas were unknown in the west; when they were discovered, the leaf difference no longer applied and the difference in the number of stamens scarcely seemed of sufficient significance to warrant the retention of a separate genus. So now *Azalea* is completely merged in *Rhododendron*, but the name is retained for one series within the genus *Rhododendron*. Some other rhododendrons have, in the past, been in a separate genus, such as *R. canadense*, which was once known as *Rhodora canadense*.

As the genus is such a large one, some further grouping

of species is necessary. Probably no other genus of flowering plant shows such diversity of form, from the 80ft tree of *R. giganteum* in the rain-soaked forests of Yunnan, to the ground-hugging mat of *R. prostratum*; from the 3ft long leaves of *R. sinogrande* to those of *R. serpyllifolium*, which just reach ⅓in; from *R. lapponicum* trailing on the arctic cliffs to tropical epiphytes such as *R. javanicum*. In the classification currently used in Britain and America, the genus (apart from the Malesian species) is divided into 44 series, each called after one of the constituent species. Some of these, like the *Griersonianum* series, contain only one species. Others, such as the *Azalea* series, are very large and are divided into several subseries. The great divide within the genus comes between those species with scales—the lepidote species—and those without scales, the elepidotes. Either group may, or may not, have hairs.

There are 23 lepidote and 21 elepidote series. The elepidotes are usually larger than the lepidotes, although there are exceptions. Although scales and hairs have a common origin, the two groups are thought to have diverged a very long time ago and to have developed on parallel lines. The scaley Triflorums, for example, resemble in many ways the elepidote azaleas. The difference does seem to be significant, as very few successful crosses have been made between a lepidote and an elepidote species, the first and best known being between *R. dalhousiae* and *R. griersonianum* to produce the hybrid 'Grierdal'. On the other hand, azaleas cross reasonably easily with other elepidote species, which underlines their unity with the rest of the genus.

Dr Sleumer, of Leiden, has proposed a revised system of classification with more subgroupings—subgenera and sections—above the series grouping. This includes the Malesian species which are out with the other system, but as yet it is not used in horticultural circles (see page 230).

The scales which have been mentioned are little structures on short stalks, often like small, flattened mushrooms. They can be seen easily with a hand lens and are usually thickest on the underside of the leaves, although they can occur elsewhere. Their function is probably that of preventing water loss by transpiration, as a layer of humid air will be trapped under the scales next to the leaf surface.

Hairs can be found in both groups. In some series, they are fine and not very obvious, but in others, such series as *Barbatum*, they are like stiff bristles. Under a microscope, hairs can be seen to be straight or branched in various ways, and the type of hair is characteristic of any one species.

Some of the series, such as *Lapponicum*, seem fairly natural groupings, with the component species having a strong family resemblance. In others, like *Campanulatum*, common characteristics are more difficult to see.

Rhododendron is not a utilitarian genus, and one, at least, of their few uses is splendidly esoteric. The woolly indumentum from the underside of the leaves of *R. lanatum* var. *luciferum* is used by the Tibetans as wicks for candles. In the past, and even now in some places, certain species had medicinal uses. Dried leaves of *R. brachycarpum* have been sold for centuries in Chinese drug shops as a treatment for circulatory disorders. Sometimes the cure seems to have been worse than the disease—Leach, in an article in the 1968 RHS *Rhododendron and Camellia Yearbook*, quotes some horrifying 'case notes'. It is always possible that orthodox use may yet be made of rhododendrons as some species, *R. maximum* for one, contain a toxic compound, Greyanotoxin I (also known as andromedotoxin and rhodotoxin). This substance has a hypotensive action, but as far as I know, has not actually been used in this way. This compound is found in other members of the Ericaceae, such as *Kalmia angustifolia*, which is known in parts of the USA as Lambkill. In Britain, leaves of *R. ponticum* can be toxic to livestock—in fact the Ponticum series seems to figure prominently in this connection. *R. maximum* and *R. bra-*

chyanthum have already been mentioned; *R. degronianum* is used to make a sort of tea in Japan, and in the next chapter there is a reference to some of the past uses of *R. chrysanthum*, one of the first species known.

The large-leaved series, *Falconeri* and *Grande*, particularly the former, are usually considered to be the most primitive, for a variety of reasons. They have the highest number of floral parts, which is biologically wasteful. The corolla may have more than 5 lobes, there may be 12–18 stamens and up to 18 chambers in the ovary. The lowest number of stamens in the genus is 5, found in most azaleas, and these are generally regarded as the most advanced and recently evolved group. These 2 primitive series are found wild only in a relatively small area from Nepal eastward through the Himalayas into Upper Burma, Yunnan and Szechwan, and they are probably the least adaptable species in the garden.

On the other hand, Almut Seithe considers, largely from a study of the hairs and scales, which are of considerable taxonomic importance, that the genus was originally deciduous. However, while of interest to botanists, this has no relevance from the horticultural point of view.

Fossil rhododendrons are known from North America. They have been found in early Tertiary rocks in Alaska, in the Trout Creek beds of eastern Oregon, and another species that is possibly a rhododendron was discovered in Pliocene deposits on Table Mountain, California.

The genus belongs predominantly to the northern hemisphere, only crossing the Equator in Indonesia, Malaya, Java and New Guinea. There is one species, *R. lochae*, in Queensland, Australia, which is related to the Java rhododendrons; there are none in Africa, Central and South America or Polynesia.

Europe has not much of a representation—9 species, and several of these just creep in around the Caucasus. There are over 40 species in the Japanese islands and North America has between 20 and 30 species, but the main centre of the genus seems to be in south-west China (Yunnan and Szechwan), Nepal and Upper Burma, where rhododendrons proliferate. I have, regrettably, never seen a rhododendron growing wild, and so can only rely on the descriptions of the great collectors, most of whom, fortunately for all lovers of the genus, were prolific with their pens.

George Forrest, who made eight plant-collecting expeditions, gathered what were at the time 309 new species of rhododendron (some have now been merged) in 30 different series, mostly in south-east Tibet and north-west Yunnan. In that area, four great rivers run north to south—the eastern branch of the Irrawaddy, the Salween, the Mekong and the Yangtse. Between latitudes 27° and 28°N these rivers run through an area less than 100 miles wide. High ranges form watersheds between them. Forrest found that not all areas were suitable for rhododendrons; most of the Mekong Valley and the Yangtse Gorge were too dry. Because of the south-west monsoon, the western slopes were a more fruitful hunting ground than the east. He describes how they grow.

> From 5,000 feet upwards, they occur as isolated specimens or small groups growing in thickets and forests of mixed dicotyledonous trees and shrubs, gradually increasing in numbers up to 10–14,000ft, at which point they form the dominant feature in the vegetation either as undergrowth in the forests of Conifers, or by themselves as dense thickets and forests. The lesser species take the place of our Heath or Calluna, carpeting miles of Alpine pasture, both above and below these forests.

Again and again, with various writers, the comparison to heather crops up. Forrest again:

> Take the moors and hills surrounding the head waters of any of our principal highland streams in the early spring, in

18

full flood, with patches of snow around. For heather and
heath, imagine mile upon mile of dwarf Rhododendron, at
that season almost the exact brownish shade of dry heather
and you have the scenery of the summit of the Bei-ma-shan
at 15,000ft.

And yet again, 'It [*R. racemosum*] holds almost the same position in the mountains of Western China as our heather does
at home.'

The distribution of many species, however plentiful they
may be in one locality, is often surprisingly limited.

> With the exception of a few species, such as *R. racemosum*,
> *R. lepidotum* and *R. decorum*, all are peculiarly local in their dis-
> tribution, in latitudinal, longitudinal and altitudinal range.
> Only a few of the species found in the Yangtse basin are com-
> mon in the areas drained by the Mekong or Salween and vice
> versa. Many of the lateral spurs of the huge ranges separating
> these basins bear species indigenous to themselves alone.

Because of these very localized distributions, it seems
highly probable that there are still species waiting to be discovered.

Forrest stresses the fact that rhododendrons are social
plants. He mentions *R. griersonianum* and *R. spinuliferum* as
exceptions to this rule, and adds . . . 'But all others are found
in masses, covering from acres to square miles in extent, and
where one species does not entirely dominate a situation
several or many have apparently adapted themselves to the
environment for the necessary mutual protection.'

Almost all rhododendrons like high humidity—one exception is *R. afghanicum*, which lives in arid areas of Afghanistan
(and would seem a possible plant for hybridizers with a view
to passing on this trait). It does not seem to be in cultivation
at present. *R. chapmanii* is also more tolerant of heat and
drought than most—it grows in sandy pine lands in Florida.

Rhododendrons in general are not very happy when the summer temperature rises above 70°F and they need a definite winter rest, except for the Malesian species which are adapted to a short day-length and an almost constant climate all the year round—this is one of the factors that complicate their cultivation.

The physical type of the plant gives some idea of its natural habitat, and following from that an indication at least, of the conditions it will like in the garden, bearing in mind that certain factors, such as a covering of snow several feet deep in winter, cannot be imitated with the best will in the world. The large-leaved species come from the temperate rain-forests, usually from between 7,000 and 9,000ft, where they grow amongst broad-leaved trees such as maples, birches, oaks and magnolias. At the top of their altitudinal range, they may be associated with conifers such as larch and silver fir.

In cultivation, these species still require tree shelter, both to break the wind and to shield them from too hot a sun, although in Britain this last is only likely to be a problem in the south.

The Triflorum series, with their small, willow-like leaves, include some of the most adaptable garden species, they come from drier and less wooded areas of central China. The dwarf, alpine types, most of the Lapponicums for example, live above the tree-line; these are the species which are buried under snow in winter. While we cannot produce this to order, winter temperatures in Britain and many parts of the USA are nothing like as severe as those in the Himalayas, and so the insulating effect of a blanket of snow is not essential. They still prefer an open situation in gardens.

In the warmer parts of their range, many rhododendrons are epiphytes. These are plants which grow, not on the ground, but on other plants. They must not be confused with parasites, however, as they do not take any food from the host plant, but simply use it as a platform to bring them nearer to the sunlight—a commodity which is in short supply below the canopy of a tropical forest. Many of these species are not invariably epiphytic; most are rather tender.

CHAPTER 2

First Introductions
and the Early Hybrids

Compared with the rose, the only genus to rival it in flower-power, the rhododendron has a relatively short garden history. The first reference to it, however, is of quite respectable antiquity. In 401 BC, Xenophon led his soldiers on the long march across Persia to the Bosphorus. In the Anabasis he wrote . . . 'All the soldiers who ate the honeycombs went out of their minds and had diarrhoea and vomiting and not a man could stand up. Those who ate only a little appeared drunk, those who had eaten a lot were like madmen, some like dying men . . . but the next day, nobody had died and they began to return to their senses.' Xenophon mentions no plant by name, but the story undoubtedly refers to the Pontic Azalea, *Rhododendron luteum*, which grows profusely in the valleys beyond Trebizond. The bees there still make their intoxicating honey, and the villagers in the area collect it and sell it in other parts of Turkey for 'medicinal purposes'.

The name rhododendron is derived from the Greek and means, literally, 'rose tree'. It was originally applied to the oleander, but in 1583, in *History of Plants* by Caesalpinus, published in Florence, the name was applied to what are now *Rhododendron ferrugineum* and *R. hirsutum*. From then until 1753, when Linnaeus established the system of binomial nomenclature in use today, and gave the name *Rhododendron* to the genus, many different names were used.

In Gerard's Herbal, published in 1597, he describes and illustrates 'Chamaerhododendros montana, Mountaine Rose Baie', which appears to be *R. ferrugineum*. 'The mountaine Rose Baie . . . growing like a little shrub, somewhat more than a cubite high, with a rough barke . . . the leaves are like the wilde Olive; on the outside green, but underneath of a rustie pale colour.'

Parkinson, in *Paradisi in Sole*, published in 1629, describes and illustrates 'Ledum Alpinum, seu Rosa alpina, the Mountaine sweet Holly Rose' and says it is 'well worthy of a fit place in our Garden'. The description is rather confused, but the accompanying picture is recognizably *R. hirsutum*.

This species is the first that is known to have been cultivated in Britain; by John Tradescant junior in Lambeth in 1656, this time as 'Balsamum alpinum, sweet mountaine rose'. The next reference to a rhododendron in cultivation is not until 1739, when Philip Miller, who was appointed to the Chelsea Garden in 1722 and remained there until 1770, is recorded as growing *R. ferrugineum*.

Miller wrote *The Gardener's Dictionary*, which went through many editions. Rhododendrons and azaleas are first mentioned in the seventh edition in 1759, but the binomial nomenclature is not used until the eighth edition in 1768, when *R. hirsutum* and *R. ferrugineum* are named as such and described. Miller says:

> There are some other species of this genus which grow naturally in the eastern countries and others are natives of America, but the two sorts here mentioned are all I have seen in English gardens; and these are difficult to propagate and

preserve in gardens, for they grow naturally upon barren rocky soils and in cold situations, where they are covered with snow a great part of the winter; so that when they are planted in better ground they do not thrive, and for want of their usual covering of snow in winter, they are frequently killed by frost; but could these plants be tamed, and propagated in plenty, they would be great ornaments to the gardens.

He goes on to describe how the seeds can be sown and grown on. Under Azalea, Miller mentions *A. viscosa*, now *R. viscosum*, and *A. nudiflora*, now *R. calendulaceum* or *R. speciosum*; all American species, introduced about 1734 by Peter Collinson, as was *R. maximum* in 1736. Of azaleas, Miller says, 'There are three or four other species of this genus, two of which grow naturally upon the Alps, chiefly on bogs; these are low plants, which have little beauty, and very difficult to keep in gardens. The others grow one in the East near Pontus, and the other in India; but as neither of these are in the English gardens, I shall not enumerate them.' *R. luteum*, to which he presumably refers, was introduced some years later, in 1793, by John Ball.

In the 1807 edition, now called *The Gardener's and Botanist's Dictionary*, with additions by Thomas Martyn, many more species are mentioned; *Rhododendrum* (sic) *ferrugineum*, *R. dauricum*, *R. chrysanthum*, *R. hirsutum*, *R. chamaecistus* (this has now been removed to another genus as *Rhodothamnus chamaecistus*), *R. ponticum*, *R. caucasicum*, *R. camtschaticum* and *R. maximum*. It is here that Martyn mentions Philip Miller as having cultivated *R. ferrugineum* in 1739. There is a long description of the medicinal powers of *R. chrysanthum*, which had evidently long been used in Siberia as a cure for rheumatism.

Little attention however was paid to it till the year 1779, when it was recommended by Koelpin not only in rheumatism and gout, but even in venereal cases; and it is now generally employed in chronic rheumatism, in various parts of Europe. The leaves, which are the part directed for medicinal use, have a bitterish sub-astringent taste, and as well as the bark and young branches, manifest a degree of acrimony. Taken in large doses they prove a narcotic poison.

The manner of using the plant by the Siberians, is by putting two drams of the dried leaves in an earthern pot, with about ten ounces of boiling water, keeping it near a boiling heat for a night: this they take in the morning, and by repeating it three or four times, generally effect a cure. It is said to occasion heat, thirst, a degree of delirium, and a peculiar sensation of the parts affected.

R. hirsutum is said to have similar medicinal effects.

R. ponticum seems to have been introduced in 1763 and *R. dauricum* in 1780 by Anthony Chaumier. *Rhodora canadense*, now *Rhododendron canadense*, is described as having been introduced in 1767 by Sir Joseph Banks. Martyn mentions the following azaleas: *A. pontica*, *A. indica*, *A. nudiflora*, *A. viscosa*, *A. lapponica*, *A. procumbens* (now *Loiseleuria procumbens*, thus depriving the British Isles of any native rhododendron) and *A. punctata* (now *R. carolinianum* or *R. minus*). It is interesting that Martyn says that a number of different colour forms of *A. viscosa* were grown, while in Curtis's Botanical Magazine, it is said of *A. nudiflora* var. *coccinea* . . . 'the Azalea coccinea was little known here till the sale of Mr. Bewick's plants in 17 [*sic*]; a considerable number of these shrubs formed the choicest part of that collection, and sold at high prices, one of them produced twenty guineas.' All this implies that in the early nineteenth century there was already quite a lot of interest in rhododendrons and azaleas as garden plants.

Martyn says that *A. pontica* and *A. indica* had not yet been cultivated in Europe, but this is certainly not true of the former. Of *A. nudiflora* and *A. viscosa* he says that they

grow naturally in shade, and upon moist ground in most parts of N America, from whence many of the plants have been sent of late years to England, and several of them have produced their beautiful flowers in many curious gardens.

They must have a moist soil and a shady situation otherwise they will not thrive. They can only be propagated by shoots from their roots, and laying down their branches, for they do not produce seeds here; and if good seeds could be obtained, they would be difficult to raise, and a long time before they would flower.

In 1808, *R. catawbiense* was discovered by John Fraser in North Carolina, and introduced to cultivation the following year. This was important, as this species was the main source of hardiness of the early 'hardy hybrids'. An even more important discovery was made in 1796, when a Captain Hardwicke, during a tour of northern India, found the first of the great tribe of Indian rhododendrons, growing on the Sewalic chain of mountains. This was soon named *R. arboreum*. Drawings were published, but seeds did not arrive in England until 1815, when Dr Wallich sent some to the Liverpool Botanic Garden.

These plants flowered ten years later, and triggered off a surge of interest in rhododendron growing and hybridizing. In the first half of the nineteenth century, a few more species trickled into cultivation, such as *R. campanulatum* and the tender *R. formosum*, but the 'great leap forward' came when Joseph Dalton Hooker collected in Sikkim in 1848 and 1849. On these two expeditions, he collected and described over 40 new species of rhododendron, more than the total in cultivation at that time. He sent drawings and descriptions to his father, Sir William Hooker, in England, who published them in the book *Rhododendrons of the Sikkim Himalaya*. This caused quite a sensation—understandably, as it included the first descriptions and illustrations of some of the most beautiful of all species, including *R. campylocarpum, R. ciliatum, R. cinnabarinum, R. falconeri, R. molle, R. griffithianum, R. maddenii, R.*

thomsonii, R. barbatum and *R. zeylanicum*. Seeds were sent to a number of gardens in Scotland and England, particularly in the south and west, and quite a few plants grown from seed from these first introductions still survive in good health and vigour.

Seeds of *R. fortunei*, a lovely species which was subsequently used a lot in hybridizing, were collected by Robert Fortune in 1855. After 1860, conditions in China became more peaceful, more ports were opened and foreigners were allowed to travel in the interior. As a result of this, more discoveries were soon made by men who were neither gardeners nor botanists, but often priests, such as Père David, or government officials like Dr Augustine Henry. The former travelled in Mongolia in 1866 and in east Szechwan in 1868 and 1869; Henry lived in central China for seven years; Delavay collected in north-west Yunnan in 1881 and Farges on the north-east border of Szechwan from 1892 to 1903; Soulié travelled on the borders of Tibet until he was shot in 1905. Some beautiful species are named after these men—*R. delavayi, R. souliei, R. augustinii, R. fargesii*; but although they found many new species, they did not always introduce them to cultivation. For example, Delavay collected 34 new species, but only 3, one of which was *R. racemosum*, were raised from seed of his collecting.

Some of the tender species also reached this country in the mid nineteenth century, such as *R. javanicum* and *R. jasminiflorum* introduced by Thomas Lobb in 1846 and the epiphytic *R. brookeanum* sent from Borneo by Hugh Low in 1845.

With the coming of the twentieth century, the flow of new species becomes too great to continue listing them. The most important collectors were E. H. Wilson (1876–1930), who collected in China and Japan; George Forrest (1873–1932), whose journeys in China covered a span of 28 years; Reginald Farrer (1880–1920), who collected in Tibet and

Burma and died there; Joseph Rock (1884–1962), who gathered almost 500 species but few new ones; Frank Ludlow and George Sheriff, who made 13 expeditions between 1933 and 1949; and Frank Kingdon-Ward (1885–1958) who first went to China in 1911 and whose last trip was to northern Burma in 1953. There is no space here to go more fully into the travels and finds of these men, as these alone could fill a book.

Many rhododendrons have been found by more than one collector and there are often considerable differences in appearance and hardiness between forms of the same species collected in different places. The *RHS Rhododendron Handbook*, Part I, 1967 edition, gives full lists of collectors' numbers, starting with Wilson's 1900–2 expedition sponsored by the nurseryman Veitch to western Hupeh, up till the Cox and Hutchison 1965 expedition to India.

The first known hybrid seems to have been what was called an Azaleodendron, an accidental cross between *R. nudiflorum* of the Azalea series, and *R. ponticum*, in the early years of the nineteenth century. To begin with, hybridizers had a very limited field to work with and followed no particular plan, but simply crossed everything that was available. Then in 1825 *R. arboreum* first flowered 'in captivity', and after that, the aim was to obtain plants with the beauty and colour of *R. arboreum* and the other Asiatic species that were gradually appearing, but also with greater hardiness and a later flowering time. Much use was made of the ultra-hardy American species *R. catawbiense* and *R. maximum*. It was found that the crosses were more successful when *R. arboreum* was used as the pollen parent than the other way around.

There seems, too, to have been a certain feeling of moral obligation involved; that it was one's duty to improve on Nature. Eduard van Regel, writing in *The Garden* magazine in 1876, said, 'Hybrids illustrate much more than the simple or primitive forms of plants. Beautiful as a plant may become when doing its best *per se*, and under the stimulus of high culture, in these we see Nature constrained to take yet another leap, transcending even the choice designs she set out with in the beginning.' *R. arboreum* he thought needed improvement not only from the point of view of hardiness, as he considered that 'the plants when out of blossom not infrequently present a lean and gloomy appearance'.

Michael Waterer was one of the first hybridizers, crossing the American species *R. maximum* and *R. catawbiense* from about 1810. The earliest hybrid mentioned in Part II of the current edition of the *Rhododendron Handbook* is 'Hybridum', a cross between *R. maximum* and *R. viscosum*, dated 1817. The dates refer to the first mention of the plant, and could be the time of flowering, raising or exhibiting. Between the years of 1804 and 1834, some important crossing was carried out in Ghent by a baker called P. Mortier. Using American species of the Azalea series, *R. arborescens, R. calendulaceum, R. nudiflorum, R. speciosum* and *R. viscosum*, and *R. luteum* from around the Black Sea, he laid the foundation of the Ghent azaleas that are still widely grown.

Most of the earliest hybrids are no longer available, having been completely superceded by modern varieties, but a few are still grown, such as the winter-flowering *R. × Nobleanum (R. arboreum × R. caucasicum*) and Jacksonii (*Nobleanum × R. caucasicum*). These two hybrids illustrate well the confusion over dates, as both are dated 1835, yet one is the parent of the other. Other old varieties that are still around include 'Fatsuosum Flore Pleno', a double mauve believed to be *R. catawbiense × R. ponticum*, and 'Lady Eleanor Cathcart', *R. arboreum × R. maximum*, dating from before 1846 and 1850 respectively.

There should be many old plants of early hybrids in existence on old estates, and doubtless there still are some, but in many cases the hybrid scion was grafted on to R. *ponticum* stock, which gradually took over, so that many of the thickets of *ponticum* that one sees around the countryside could have started life originally as hybrid plantings.

As more and more species came into cultivation, the range of hybrids increased also. Some crossing was still carried out haphazardly, but more and more, breeders aimed at a specific goal, either a certain colour, or habit of plant, or time of flowering. It seems to take a very long time, perhaps half a century, for a variety to become really widely available. The type of rhododendron predominantly seen today is still the 'hardy hybrid'— plants such as Cynthia, Sappho and Pink Pearl—and most of these were bred around or before the turn of the century. Cynthia, indeed, was released on the market in 1860. These plants, while often opulent of flower, are notably undistinguished of form and foliage. There are many newer hybrids which are much more elegant and no more difficult to grow, but these are still not always easy to obtain.

CHAPTER 3

Garden Requirements

Most people with any interest in gardening beyond cutting the grass must know that there are some soils in which rhododendrons and azaleas will not grow. These are soils derived from chalk and limestone; like most other members of the Ericaceae, rhododendrons will only grow in acid soil.

Soil acidity is expressed in terms of pH, which is a measure of the hydrogen ion concentration. A hydrogen ion is a hydrogen atom which has lost an electron and thus become positively charged. An acid is defined as a substance which dissociates to form hydrogen ions, and so the more there are of the latter, the greater is the acidity. The pH scale is a logarithmic one, and so if a solution has a concentration of 10^{-3}g-ions per litre, its pH is said to be equal to 3. As the index is negative, the lower the number, the greater the acidity. The scale runs up to 14, with pH 7 being neutral, anything over that being alkaline and below 7 being acid. A solution (or soil) of pH 6 is ten times as acid as one of pH 7; one of pH 5 is ten times as acid as pH 6 and one hundred times more acid than pH 7.

In general, rhododendrons can only be grown successfully in soils having an acidity greater than pH 6; probably about

5 is the optimum value. pH is easy to measure, it is possible to buy soil-testing kits, where acidity is estimated by comparing the colour obtained with a standard chart.

Alkalinity in soils is almost always linked with the presence of calcium carbonate. As chalk and limestone are almost pure calcium carbonate, these soils have high pH values. A high pH can, however, be caused by other chemicals. Dr Henry Tod, of the Edinburgh School of Agriculture, made up soils with pH values up to 8, using magnesium carbonate to produce the alkalinity, and successfully grew seedlings of *R. davidsonianum* in them for two or three years. This suggests that it is not the alkalinity as such that is harmful to rhododendrons, but large amounts of calcium. Certainly no rhododendron could survive in a soil of pH 8, where that was caused by calcium salts.

Rhododendrons, like other plants, need some calcium to keep in good health, but it seems that when large quantities are present, the calcium is taken up in preference to the closely related chemical magnesium, with the result that the latter becomes deficient. (This is rather similar to the way in which human bones will make use of strontium 90 instead of calcium, if that isotope is present in radioactive fallout.) Iron also becomes deficient in the presence of excess lime, because of the formation of insoluble iron compounds which the plant is then unable to use. This particular effect is by no means confined to rhododendrons and their allies; it is well known in many fruit crops.

It is possible to get magnesian limestones, such as dolomite, where the rock is a mixture of calcium and magnesium carbonate. If sufficient magnesium is present, rhododendrons may well be able to take in enough for their needs, in spite of the presence of calcium. This type of rock is found in parts of the north of England and in the far north of Scotland.

There have been many reports of rhododendrons in the

wild growing on limestone. George Forrest, searching for plants in Yunnan, described seeing *R. chartophyllum* and its form *praecox*, flowering profusely, growing on pure limestone, sometimes apparently on the bare rock. It seems probable that in such cases as this, the limestone must contain a high proportion of magnesium and also, the high rainfall would lead to rapid leaching of salts. As far as I know, Forrest sent back no rock or soil samples—in fact there have been very few soil analyses of sites in the wild. Some species, notably *R. hirsutum*, *R. lapponicum* and *R. calciphilum*, do seem to grow mainly on limestone and this would seem a field worth the consideration of hybridizers.

Garden soil may have an alkaline reaction for one of two reasons. First, because the soil is derived from chalk or limestone, in which case little can be done. If, however, the soil is alkaline because the previous owner had limed the garden, the alkalinity should eventually disappear, more quickly in an area of high rainfall than in a dry part of the country. It is worth adding Epsom salts (magnesium sulphate) at the rate of 2oz (1 tablespoonful) per gallon of water, or iron sequestrene according to the directions on the packet, to hasten the process. In our present garden, which is on Greensand, we were alarmed to find lots of little lumps of chalk about the size of a fingernail rising to the surface. Their presence was explained when a neighbour told us that the previous owner had applied mushroom compost, which contains chalk, to the beds. The pieces have to picked out by hand, but in the end the garden should be none the worse.

Even in chalky districts, it is possible to find the odd pocket where dead leaves and other decaying vegetation have built up to form a layer of acid soil of sufficient depth to allow rhododendrons to grow. This will often be on top of a hill, where there is no seepage of chalky water from higher ground. There are rhododendrons growing on top of Box

Hill in Surrey, which is virtually a lump of solid chalk. One can get a fair idea of what the soil of an area is like by noticing what other people are able to grow in their gardens, and the natural vegetation of a district is also a good indicator of soil conditions. As far as I know, the wild clematis *C. vitalba*, Old Man's Beard or Traveller's Joy, is completely confined to alkaline soils, and where it festoons the hedgerows, rhododendrons cannot grow. Wild heathers and heaths indicate acid soils, and so usually does bracken. Rushes and sallows are a sign of poor drainage.

High rainfall and low temperatures slow down the breakdown of organic matter by bacteria and fungi, and this leads to the formation of an acid soil. This is one of the reasons why, in the wild, rhododendrons are predominantly plants of mountain areas—mountains attract rain, and the average annual temperature decreases by $1°F$ for every 300ft rise in altitude. It is also part of the reason why, in the British Isles, the west coast is in general more suitable for rhododendron growing than the east.

I do not think it is worth the struggle to grow rhododendrons on soils that are definitely alkaline. If the soil is borderline, say pH 6–7, then Epsom salts, peat, sequestrene and ferrous sulphate may do the trick. Ferrous sulphate is useful for increasing soil acidity—sulphur can also be used, but as it is toxic in excess, it is better avoided. Adding ferrous sulphate does not increase the amount of iron available, as the iron becomes locked up as insoluble ferric hydroxide, but calcium sulphate is formed, which is highly soluble, and so leaches out of the soil. Either crystals of ferrous sulphate can be scattered round the base of the plants in question, or a saturated solution can be made up in a watering can and watered on to the soil. If this is done, it is important not to let the solution touch the leaves, as it turns them black. It may be necessary to repeat the treatment a few times.

34

In a strongly alkaline soil, some of the dwarf and prostrate forms can be grown in raised peat beds. These are made by building walls from well-soaked peat blocks, in the manner of a dry-stone wall, and filling in behind with a suitable peat and loam mixture. The beds must be carefully sited, so that there is no risk of alkaline water draining into them from higher ground. Watering is likely to be a problem, however. Raised beds tend to dry out quickly and most districts with alkaline soil will also have alkaline tap water, although this is not always the case as water is sometimes piped from a considerable distance. (The converse can also occur, with tap water being more alkaline than the soil.) Any watering should be done with rain water, which can be collected in butts. Evergreen azaleas and other dwarfs look well in tubs, and the frustrated enthusiast could also grow some like this.

It is not easy to know just how deeply to go into the subject of soil and mineral deficiency. Clearly, one could go on at great length and in great detail, but this tends to have rather the same effect on the reader as does working through a medical encyclopedia—he thinks he has got the lot. Rhododendron ailment diagnosis is further complicated by the fact that so often the endpoint is the same although the cause may be different—namely chlorosis.

Chlorosis is the term given to a yellowing of the leaf, caused by a lack of chlorophyll. Chlorophyll is the green pigment found in all plants except a few parasites. By means of this substance, in the presence of sunlight, plants are able to photosynthesize, that is to manufacture sugars and starches from atmospheric carbon dioxide and the water in the cells and intercellular spaces. The commonest cause of chlorosis is lack of magnesium or iron or both. Magnesium is an actual part of the chlorophyll molecule, and iron is necessary for its formation, so if either of these is unavailable, the leaves will be yellowish in colour instead of a healthy green, and the plant will eventually die. There may well be plenty of iron and magnesium present in the soil, but if there is also a lot of calcium rhododendrons and other ericaceous plants will be unable to make use of them. Plants can only take in nutrients in a soluble form and if an element is locked up in an insoluble salt, it cannot be used. Organic fertilizers release nutrients more slowly than 'artificials', but the chemicals involved are the same.

Magnesium deficiency is by no means confined to calcareous soils; it occurs not uncommonly on acid soils, and this possibility should be kept in mind if rhododendrons growing on a soil with a low pH become chlorosed. Again, Epsom salts can be used to correct this.

Apart from its peculiarities regarding calcium, the metabolism of rhododendrons is similar to that of other plants. The major plant nutrients are nitrogen, phosphorus, potassium, calcium and magnesium, and the minor ones are iron, manganese, sulphur, boron, copper and zinc. Some other elements are needed in minute traces.

Nitrogen controls the amount of growth that a plant makes. With excess nitrogen, it will become lush and dark green, with more leaf than flower; with too little, it will be pale and stunted. Phosphates help fruit and seed production and promote root growth. If phosphorus is deficient, the leaves become dull and reddish blotches may appear. Acid soils are quite often lacking in phosphorus; ammonium phosphate is suitable for correcting this.

If nitrogen has to be supplied, it should be given as part of the ammonium radicle, eg as ammonium sulphate, and not in nitrate form, as that radicle is able to combine with metallic ions and form alkaline salts.

Potassium is necessary for good foliage, and if it is deficient, the leaves may appear scorched round the margins and will eventually fall. Manganese deficiency can lead to chlorosis, as it is linked to the assimilation of iron; but it must be added only in very small quantities (as manganese sulphate) for, if it is present in excess, it will displace iron.

In considering fertilizers, any which contain calcium in any form, such as bone-meal, nitro-chalk or superphosphates, should be avoided. Potassium fertilizers are often alkaline. Chopped green bracken and banana skins are a useful and harmless source of potassium. In general, apart from the provision of iron and magnesium, it is advisable to use organic fertilizers rather than artificials, as with the latter it is very easy to get an imbalance of nutrients, quite apart from the risk of inducing a high pH. Dried blood is good, particularly for free-flowering types such as *R. thomsonii*. It has a horrid smell but that does not last for long. Hoof-and-horn is also good. Like most plants, rhododendrons respond well to foliar feeding. Cold tea leaves, which have a pH of about 5·4, are a good tonic. They can be collected in a bucket, or added to the compost heap, or simply emptied from the pot (after filling it up with *cold* water) at the base of those plants growing near the house.

If sharp sand is added to lighten the soil and improve drainage, it should not be sea shore sand as this would almost certainly contain pieces of shell, which are calcareous. One is advised not to apply ash to rhododendrons and particularly not to plant them where there has been a fire. Kingdon-Ward and others have described seeing seedlings growing in such an area, but this could be because the vegetation which had been growing in that area would be likely to contain an extremely low level of calcium and the high rainfall would lead to rapid leaching. In gardens, ash and bonfire sites are better avoided.

Rhododendrons thrive on soils which contain a lot of humus. This is decaying organic matter, and may be applied as leaf-mould, farmyard manure (not poultry), garden compost (as long as it does not contain egg-shells or too many cabbage stalks), peat or rotted pine-needles. Oak and beech leaf-mould is supposed to be the richest in nutrients, but it must not come from trees growing on chalk or limestone, or this will be reflected in a high calcium content. Leaf-mould and manure should always be well rotted, as otherwise nitrogen deficiency will arise, because of the needs of the bacteria that break down organic matter. Sawdust should be avoided for the same reason. From the structural aspect, humus of any kind helps to keep the soil well aerated, which improves a clay soil, and also increases a soil's powers of water retention, which is advantageous in a sandy soil. The ideal rhododendron soil is moist, yet well drained, so neither a very sandy nor a very clayey soil is suitable without treatment.

Speaking of clay soils leads to the subject of new gardens. Very often, particularly when an estate of new houses is built, the top soil is removed by the builders and, whatever they may say in their brochures, is not replaced. As a result, the prospective gardener is faced with a sea of glutinous clay. Ideally, one would bring in new topsoil but this is rarely practicable because of the cost, and so the soil, as it exists, has to be improved. Any organic matter is, of course, useful, but this eventually rots down. One answer is to order a load of *weathered* boiler ash, spread it 3 or 4in thick over the surface of the soil, and fork it into at least the top foot. It must be well weathered, to be sure that any potentially harmful soluble salts have been washed out. This should improve aeration and drainage to quite a marked extent. In the process of forking over, any odd bits of cement, mortar, old bricks etc should, of course, be removed. Once the area of the lawn and the shape of the beds have been laid out, the exact positions of the plants can be decided. The planting hole needs to be well dug out, and peat or other humus should be mixed in. I see no reason why rhododendrons should not be grown in the gardens of new houses, as long as they are carefully chosen. The old hardy hybrids are too large and bulky, although one could be useful as a windbreak. Many of the taller species require more shelter than would be commonly found on a new estate, but many of the medium to dwarf species and compact modern hybrids are very suitable.

Rhododendron roots do not spread very deeply or widely, but remain near the surface, forming a compact root-ball. This is why rhododendrons can be moved at any time of year, as long as care is taken not to disturb the root-ball. In fact, if a rhododendron is not thriving in a garden, and treatment of the soil seems to have no effect, it is always worth moving it to another site. In our garden, there are several plants which had to be moved two or three times before they seemed happy.

Rhododendrons should never be planted deeply—this is a common cause of their languishing. They should not be planted more deeply than they were in the nursery where they were bought—the mark can usually be seen easily enough on the stem. The ground beneath rhododendrons should not be hoed because of the risk of damage to the roots—in any case it should not be necessary, as the plants should be kept mulched. This should be done at least once a year, preferably twice, in spring and autumn. A mulch protects the roots from cold in winter and from excessive heat in summer, and helps to conserve soil moisture, which is even more important. It is best to apply a mulch when the soil is already wet. It should not be of a claggy material (like sawdust) but light, so that air can still reach the roots. Peat, leaf-mould and chopped green bracken are all good. These will gradually rot down into the soil so that the mulch does not mount higher and higher up the stem.

When a rhododendron is being planted or replanted, a

hole should be dug out considerably larger than the size of the root-ball, and peat or leaf-mould should be mixed into the soil. If this is not done, the roots may be reluctant to leave the favourable area of the root-ball and extend into the hard, unfriendly medium outside it.

Soil is by no means the only factor to be considered in growing rhododendrons. Wind shelter is vitally important. In general, the larger the leaf, the more shelter is needed. Wind affects rhododendrons adversely in two ways. First of all, it can cause mechanical damage, and this is where the magnificent leathery leaves of the giants are so susceptible. Then it has a drying effect—provided the relative humidity is less than 100 per cent, the loss of water through the leaves by transpiration will always be greater in a wind, as in still weather a locally humid atmosphere will build up around the leaves, thus decreasing the transpiration rate. This effect is suffered to some extent by all rhododendrons (indeed by all plants), but many do not require so much humidity. Kingdon-Ward makes the point that 'It is drought far more than heat or cold, which kills rhododendrons.'

In a large garden, the provision of shelter is no problem, as tree shelter is the best of all—light woodland is ideal. But big rhododendrons must not be planted too closely, or much of their beauty will be lost. For the many who cannot provide a small copse, it is often possible, even in a small garden, to make use of existing trees and hedges, or the wall of a house or garage, to give shelter from the prevailing wind. It is important to avoid wind tunnels, or the sort of blustery corner where the wind comes gusting round the side of a house. In fact a broken windbreak, such as is formed by trees or bushes, is to be preferred to a solid one such as a wall. A solid windbreak gives shelter for a distance roughly equal to its height, but at the edge of this there is usually an area of turbulence. This can be avoided by having a broken windbreak, where the wind can filter through, and the area of protection given is considerably greater relative to height.

Apart from the alpine species, few rhododendrons like full exposure to the sun, except in places where light intensity is not high, as there are frequent clouds, as in Scotland and British Columbia, and the Dunedin area of New Zealand. On the other hand, some sunshine is needed to ripen the new wood, which will bear the following season's flower-buds (except for *R. camtschaticum*, which flowers on the current season's wood). In too dense a shade, rhododendrons become drawn up and leggy, but too much sun can fade or brown the flowers. The nearest thing to a happy medium seems to be the dappled shade provided by small trees. It may well be advisable in a very exposed part of the country to make sure that this is present before the rhododendrons are planted—although few people now would emulate Osgood Mackenzie, who waited for thirty years after putting in his shelter-belts before he began serious planting at Inverewe. If shade and shelter are impossible to provide, it is best to concentrate on the dwarfs.

Hardiness in rhododendrons is a strange thing. The *RHS Rhododendron Handbook* gives all species in general cultivation a rating for hardiness and constitution.

H4: hardy anywhere in the British Isles.

H3: hardy in the south and west, and along the seaboard and in sheltered gardens inland.

H2: requires protection in the most sheltered gardens.

H1: a species which can usually be grown only as a greenhouse plant.

This is not quite as straightforward as it might seem, as certain species are notoriously variable in their hardiness, and this seems to depend from which part of its range the original plant came. The offspring of plants from a high altitude are usually considerably hardier than those of plants from a lower level, even in the same species. All too often, the most striking forms seem to be the least hardy, as in *R. arboreum* (which has a RHS rating of H2–4), where the blood-red forms are more tender than the pink, and in *R. augustinii* where the form with the bluest flowers is the least hardy.

To be sure of getting a hardy form, it is best to deal with a reputable nursery, preferably one located in a slightly colder part of the country. In the United States, species and hybrids hardy anywhere in the British Isles can generally be grown along the west coast. Rhododendrons which can be grown along the east coast must be able to stand summer heat as well as winter cold.

South of Washington DC on the east coast, summer heat is the limiting factor, with the occurrence of certain root rots that are much more prevalent in southern areas. There are certain varieties, mostly hardy hybrids, that are known to be heat resistant, for example Blue Peter, Cynthia, Gomer Waterer, Purple Splendour and among dwarfs, Blue Tit. Even these should be planted where they get virtually no direct sunlight, especially in the middle of the day.

The 1967 edition of the *Rhododendron Handbook* is currently being revised and there are likely to be alterations to both ratings and classification. However, those given are what is available at the time of writing.

The American Rhododendron Society has its own rating system. This gives in degrees Fahrenheit (in 5 degree steps) the minimum temperature which a mature plant is likely to be able to withstand without visible damage. This does not count damage which may be caused by a snap frost after a period of growth.

The time of year when a cold spell occurs can be important. If the weather grew gradually colder until January or February, and then gradually warmer again until spring, life would be much easier. Unfortunately frosty spells can come with no warning, either in early autumn before the summer growth has properly hardened, or in late spring after the sap has started flowing. Frost at either of these times is much more damaging than low winter temperatures—after all, species growing wild in the Himalayas and their foothills undergo much lower temperatures than they ever would in the British Isles, although the small ones would have their insulating snow blanket. The next season's flower-buds are formed towards the end of summer and in autumn, and are usually not affected by frost until they start to swell in spring, but a snap autumn frost is occasionally damaging.

It is reasonable to assume, in most gardens, that any rhododendron that flowers in April or earlier is liable to be frosted, but many beautiful species and hybrids come into this class, and as flowers are especially welcome at this time of year, it would be a pity to ban them all from the garden. While we cannot control the weather, we can do a certain amount to ameliorate its effects. Cold air is heavier than warm, and so frost tends to flow downhill. If there is a free passage for it, such as through a thin hedge or open gateway, or slatted fence, it will roll on somewhere else. But if its exit from the garden is blocked, a frost pocket is formed. If nothing can be done about this, that part of the garden must be kept for ultra-hardy, late-flowering plants. For plants that might be frosted, one of the higher parts of the garden should be chosen. Even a small garden often has variations in level, so this does not concern only owners of large areas.

There are some other ways of trying to minimize frost damage to an early flowering plant. It can be planted at the base of a wall—the wall of a house in particular is often several degrees warmer than surrounding objects. Another method is to give it a certain amount of tree shelter, as a light canopy of branches can cut out a slight frost. Alternatively, an early flowerer—most are hardy *in themselves*, it is the flowers and buds that are at risk—can be planted in full exposure, in a north-facing situation, in an attempt to retard flowering by a couple of weeks. One usually reads that these varieties should not be grown where they will catch the early morning sun, that is to say, facing east, as sometimes if a bud can thaw out slowly it will be unaffected whereas if the frost is suddenly thawed, the bud will be ruined. I have not noticed this effect myself, but it is worth bearing in mind. It is curious that some flowers, such as those of the camellia 'Donation', can come through hard frosts unscathed, while rhododendron flowers, which are not so different in texture, can stand no frost at all.

In New Zealand and those parts of Australia where rhododendrons are grown, such as the Melbourne area, early flowering is often an advantage. There, sun damage is a problem and the early flowerers have their show over before the hottest time of the year. The rhododendron season in these parts of the southern hemisphere has its peak in October and early November and finishes in December. Imported plants seem to adapt to the change of season surprisingly quickly, in a matter of months. Later flowering types such as *R. griersonianum* and its hybrids must be given shade from the afternoon sun.

In the Melbourne area and much of New Zealand, as well as in the San Francisco area of the United States, many species and hybrids that are cool-house plants in Britain grow well outside, for example *R. maddenii*, *R. nuttallii*, Princess Alice, Countess of Haddington and Fragrantissimum. *R. williamsianum*, on the other hand, appears to lack sun-hardiness as well as frost hardiness. In the Melbourne area, some of the New Guinea rhododendrons grow well outside and are, as might be expected, very heat resistant. *R. laetum*, *R. javanicum*, *R. konori*, *R. christianae* and *R. gracilentum* are among those which have been tried successfully.

44

The southern end of South Island, New Zealand, as far up the east coast as Canterbury, can have frost in the 3 winter months. In Dunedin, near the southern tip of the island, many rhododendrons flower better in full sun than in shade, but in Christchurch, some 226 miles further north, rhododendrons must have shade to be successful.

In a different category from the early-flowering species are those where the whole plant is slightly tender. Obviously, with so many species and hybrids which are bone hardy to choose from, there is no need to grow these at all. But many are very beautiful, and few gardeners can resist the attempt to grow something that is perhaps just beyond the limit of what could reasonably be expected to be hardy. The usual way is to grow such a plant in the shelter of light woodland, if one is lucky enough to have such a site at one's disposal. The opulent and lovely *R. griffithianum*, one of the most exotic looking plants that can be grown outside anywhere in the British Isles, has to be grown in this way even in the south and west. With some plants, though, another way that sometimes succeeds is, paradoxically, to grow the plant in question in full exposure, relying on the sun to really harden the wood. *R. griersonianum* is rated H3–4, and is generally considered to be tender, particularly when young, but we have (so far) been successful in growing it fully exposed, it flowers profusely each year and has as yet been quite unscathed by frost.

When the temperature is below freezing point, the leaves of many rhododendrons—*R. thomsonii* for one—roll up like cinnamon sticks. There is nothing to be alarmed at in this; when the thermometer rises again, the leaves will uncurl and be none the worse.

There are now available both in the UK and the USA, substances which can only be described as 'anti-freeze' for plants. One of these is called PVP/VA S-630, and is sold as a 1–5

45

per cent solution of the substance in water. This is sprayed on to the foliage and appears to lower the freezing-point of the cell solutions which enables the plant to withstand lower temperatures than it otherwise could. The same substance, again when sprayed on the leaves, helps to prevent wilting after transplanting or during the winter months, when more water is being lost by transpiration than can be taken in through the roots. I have not tried this out, and so have no personal experience of its efficacy.

While one can generalize about the correct situation for a rhododendron (or any other plant), plants are living organisms, and therefore not always predictable. It can be depressing to read that a certain plant, apparently healthy and thriving, is in the completely wrong situation. At one time, I used to move the plant in question, and all too often it languished and died in its ideal new environment. Now, I would never move a healthy plant unless it was growing too big for its site, but would be ready to do so if it started struggling. Fine plants have been known to grow in improbable situations. This does not mean that one should not try to provide the right conditions, if they are known, for a new plant; it is simply a counsel to leave well alone.

Few plants need as little maintenance as rhododendrons— the annual ritual of pruning, for example, is quite undesirable. Dead-heading, while not essential, does help to give a better display the following year. To be effective, it should be done as soon as the flowers have faded, as the longer the seeds have been allowed to develop, the less benefit, if any, there will be from the operation. If it is wanted to save some seed, one or two pods can be left on. In nature, many rhododendrons, like other plants, might flower only in alternate years, especially if the display was very extravagant in the years it occurred. Dead-heading should encourage annual flowering. Obviously, in a large collection or where individual plants are very large, it may not be practicable. In such a case, the gardener should do what he can, and not worry about what he cannot do. No permanent harm is likely to befall the plants.

Climate, of course, poses different problems in different parts of the country. While some places are more windy than others, the means taken to protect against wind will be the same—it is just that some have to take them more rigorously. In a really exposed garden, where it is impossible to give adequate protection, the only solution may be to concentrate on dwarf species and hybrids and to get the height needed for the design of the garden from other, more wind-hardy plants.

The other obvious adverse factor is, of course, cold, and here it would seem on first sight that the further north one goes, the more difficult life becomes. This does not necessarily follow, as in the north there is much less likelihood of false springs. In the south, one or two winter months can pass with no frost, plants are tempted into precocious growth, and when a frost comes—as it surely will—much more damage is done than if the temperature had been uniformly low. When one reads of what is grown in various parts, the reaction is that almost anything can be grown anywhere by someone who is prepared to take a bit of trouble. This, of course, is exaggerated, but I certainly think that the scope of certain plants is not as limited as is often thought.

Edinburgh is not the most clement part of the British Isles, yet the Royal Botanic Gardens there has an outstanding collection of rhododendrons, growing out of doors. In the survey *Rhododendron in the North*, published by the Northern Horticultural Society, covering 32 gardens in the north of England and the south of Scotland, only 6 series were not represented—*Albiflorum*, *Camelliaeflorum*, *Ovatum*, *Semibarbatum*, *Stamineum* and *Vaccinioides*. The first of these is not, as

47

far as I know, in cultivation in Britain, and the others are all tender and not much grown anywhere. *R. bullatum* and *R. edgeworthii*, 8 members of the Falconeri series, 5 of the Grande series and 8 of the Maddenii series were listed, although of the last, only *R. crassum*, *R. ciliatum* and *R. fletcheranum* were reported as being fairly hardy. Nearly all the other planting reports referred to one mild woodland garden near the sea. With the Falconeri series, the difficulty seems to be to get them to flower in the north. I have a report of one in Aberdeen that is estimated to be 40 years old, looks well and is about 12 ft high, that has never flowered, and in *Rhododendron in the North*, *R. fictolacteum* is mentioned as not having flowered at 32 years and *R. hodgsonii* only once in 30 years. One certainly does not have to wait as long as that in the south of England—our *R. falconeri* first flowered at about 8 years old, and I know of a *R. rex* that flowers well at about 10 years old, but with these plants, the foliage is as attractive as the flowers.

In Aberdeen, *R. sinogrande* and *R. macabeanum* are reported as having been killed by frost after a number of years' growth, but *R. × loderi* 'Pink Diamond' and *R. × loderi* 'King George' do well there. Sub-zero (Fahrenheit) temperatures are by no means rare in Aberdeen.

On the whole, the best advice would seem to be to have a framework of species and hybrids which are known to be hardy, and then to be prepared to experiment a bit.

Snow lying on branches can break them off, and rhododendrons, like other evergreens are vulnerable to this. All that can be done is to get out as quickly as possible and shake off the snow from as many branches as can be reached.

If a branch has been split, but not completely broken off, by snow or wind or any other reason, it is worth tying it back into place with string or twine, using another sound branch to support it if necessary. The string should be checked from time to time to make sure that the broken part is still held tightly in place. Sometimes this works and sometimes it does not, but it is always worth the attempt if a branch which, if cut off, would spoil the look of the plant, has been damaged.

Another winter effect which is not peculiar to rhododendrons—I think primulas are the worst sufferers—is the way that roots are lifted out of the soil after a frost. In rhododendrons this only happens to young plants, particularly seedlings, and it is a good idea after a frosty spell to check that the plants are still firmly in the ground.

The roots of rhododendrons are always associated with a fungus, a relationship known as mycorrhiza. This relationship is quite common in plants which grow in humus-rich soil; it is found in most members of the Ericaceae, in orchids, and in many forest trees, such as beech. Some authorities consider that the fungus is simply a parasite, if not a very harmful one, on the higher plant, but the usual theory is that both partners gain from the association, with the larger plant benefiting from the breakdown products of the fungus's action on the humus, and the fungus presumably gaining other plant foods from the host. How essential the fungus is to rhododendrons is not yet known. The seeds of many orchids will not grow without the presence of the appropriate fungus, unless a complete nutrient solution is provided, which suggests that the fungus does supply something that the higher plant needs. Any rhododendron bought from a nursery can be presumed to have the necessary fungi already present in its root-ball, and it does not seem likely that lack of mycorrhiza is a factor which commonly causes the failure of rhododendrons in a garden, but I suppose it is a possibility. It is a subject about which there is still a great deal to be learned.

GREENHOUSE RHODODENDRONS

Why do people grow rhododendrons in greenhouses, when there would seem to be plenty of species and hybrids that grow easily out of doors? Many of these tender kinds have an opulence of flower and a heavy fragrance rarely found in the hardier types. Species such as *R. nuttallii*, with white or pale yellow trumpets as much as 6in across and glossy brown bark, and *R. rhabdotum*, with 4in long funnel-shaped, creamy white blooms, flushed with yellow inside and red-striped outside, have flowers beautiful enough to make people willing to go to quite a lot of trouble in order to grow them.

Rhododendrons have been grown in warm greenhouses since about the middle of the nineteenth century, and the fact that their requirements were slightly different from those of 'ordinary' rhododendrons was recognized even then. Hugh Low, who collected in the far east about that time, said in a book on Sarawak, '. . . the roots of the Rhododendrons, instead of being, as with the species, inhabitants of cold climates, small and fibrous, become large and fleshy, winding round the trunks of the forest trees; the most beautiful is that which I have named in compliment to Mr. Brooke.' This was *R. brookeanum*. It and *R. javanicum* and *R. jasminiflora* and a few other Javan and Malayan species were grown and also used to breed many greenhouse hybrids. Much of this was done by James Veitch and Sons of Chelsea, who also introduced many of the species.

Now, these warm house subjects are not grown much. More popular are those that can be grown in cool greenhouses, where the winter temperature may fall to about 30°F. Some of these are species which are quite hardy outside, but flower so early that more often than not, the buds are damaged by frost, for example *R. moupinense* and *R. leucaspis*, which flower in February and March. Outside, it is frustrating to watch the flower-buds slowly enlarging, only to see them soggy and brown after an unexpected night's frost at the vital moment. Many cool greenhouse species come from the lower reaches of the Himalayas, such as *R. dalhousiae* and *R. edge-worthii*. A number of species of the Maddenii series that may be hardy outside in favoured gardens are more usually grown under cover.

As can be seen from the description of rhododendrons growing in Sarawak, many of these tender species are epiphytes and virtually all are forest plants, growing in the wild in shady and humid situations. This gives a clue to the way in which they should be treated. They must have plenty of water in the growing season, although very little in winter, and should be sprayed frequently. From time to time, foliar feed can be added to the spray. Plenty of ventilation is required and, in summer, they should be shaded during hot spells.

All rhododendrons like a well drained and well aerated compost, and this is even more necessary for these epiphytic species. They can be grown in beds, in pots or even in slatted, hanging baskets, like orchids. Pots can be stood outside in summer and should always have two or three inches of rubble in the bottom.

A suitable soil mixture is made up of equal parts of peat, lime-free loam and coarse sand. Some leaf-mould may be substituted for part of the loam. The warm greenhouse types need an even more open compost, for example one made of equal parts of peat and sphagnum moss.

Some mention should be made of what are called the Malesian rhododendrons, although as almost all of them are unobtainable in commerce, their interest is purely theoretical for most of us. These are species, mainly from New Guinea and Borneo, many of which have been discovered in the past thirty years. Most of the work of classification has been done by Dr H. Sleumer, who has recognized almost 300 species. He has divided them into five sections, but only one of these, *Vireya* (which includes the Javanicum series), has members in cultivation.

It seems likely that there are many potential greenhouse species amongst this group, but as yet very little is known about their cultivation. In the wild, they are adapted to short day-lengths throughout the year, in fact there is only about thirty minutes' difference between the longest and the shortest day, and they are not subject to any winter resting period. They grow at altitudes varying from 400 to 13,500ft and some, according to the height at which they grow, may prove to be cool rather than warm greenhouse subjects. *R. lochae*, Australia's only native rhododendron, found in northern Queensland, did in fact receive an Award of Merit in 1957 as a cool greenhouse plant.

A list of species and hybrids suitable for greenhouse cultivation is given at the end of the book.

Rhododendrons growing in a
photograph includes *R. neriiflo*
and *R. campylocarpum*. The tre
a 'C

mound of 'Elizabeth' or
too, in the shapes and c
long, dark almost lineai
are nearly round and l
glaucous blue ones, whil
long, dark and leathery
are deciduous, but they l
leafless, and often give a
when the leaves turn red

Tall Species for the Back of
The tall species of rhoc
a border, where they

on permanent plantings of trees, shrubs and herbaceous plants. This is labour saving, at least once the plants have become established. Few people now have help in the garden, and no one wants to spend so much time working in a garden that he has no time to enjoy it. Furthermore, a garden of this style can be attractive at all times of the year if use is made of contrasts of form and foliage and there is a framework of evergreens. A garden based on bedding plants may be a blaze of colour throughout much of the year, but one still looks out of the window in winter.

As far as colour is concerned, flowers in general can be classified into 3 groups. Group 1 has no blue; this would include roses and chrysanthemums. Group 2 has no reds, for example, irises. Group 3 has no yellows; this includes plants such as sweet peas and brooms. Most of the elepidote rhododendrons belong to group 1. The nearest to blue is probably found in some forms of *R. campanulatum*. This is why the hardy hybrids, which are crosses of elepidote species, contain nothing nearer blue than the lavender of Susan or Blue Peter.

The Obtusum subseries of azaleas, which are also elepidote, could be said to belong to group 3. These plants, the evergreen azaleas and their hybrids, have colours in the white–pink–red–magenta colour range.

The lepidote series belong to group 2. Although rhododendrons can be said to include all groups, there is no clear blue in the genus; even the best form of *R. augustinii* has tones of violet. So to bring blue into the garden, which almost every gardener wants to do, one must turn to other plants.

In the spring, of course, there are blues in plenty from dwarf bulbs such as scillas and chionodoxas and later on, bluebells. These look particularly well with dwarf yellow rhododendrons, whether it is the greenish-yellow of the March and April flowering Bo-peep, or the vivid yellow of Chikor in April and May. *Brunnera macrophylla* has forget-me-not

55

flowers and larg
Later on, *Mecon*
wards the end of
soils that rhodo

Virtually all
drons, and cho
a matter of taste
crimson, scarle
blends. Magent
difficult colours
ring effect on
complement; th
gether. Persona
in its commone
table magenta,
it with the cle
other rhododer
very attractive.

Yellow, in fa
in it, is an in
to be nothing
is ample choice
in spring to s
later in the yea
useful plant, w
as well as its p

Rhododend
garden. When
rivalled by few
iety, the flowe
people think—
in flower in e
most are ever
of the plant, fi

R. rex is one of the hardiest of the large-leaved, tree rhododendrons. This specimen was growing in quite a small town garden. One of the leaves in the foreground shows the effects of vine-weevil damage.

shelter from a fence, hedge or wall. Everyone who enjoys rhododendrons would like to grow at least one of the tree species, which are amongst the most splendid plants of any genus that can be grown in a temperate garden. Unfortunately, they are not suited to every garden as some, although not all, are slightly tender, but all must have wind shelter, as explained in the previous chapter. These large-leaved species need plenty of moisture and are generally at their best in places such as the west of Britain, the Pacific coast of the USA, western coastal areas of New Zealand and places such as the Dadenong Hills near Melbourne. In drier and colder districts some, such as *R. fictolacteum* and *R. rex* will grow well enough, but their leaves will be smaller—even so, they are still fine plants. If there is a garden pond of any size it is

R. calophytum, like many rhododendrons—species in particular—is as attractive in its new growth as in flower.

a good idea to plant a large-leaved species beside it, as atmospheric humidity will be higher near the water. In any case, they should be given as much water as is possible while they are making growth.

The new growth can be one of the most attractive features of many rhododendrons, when the young leaves are silvery or whitish, as in *R. calophytum* and *R. lanatum.* Sometimes there are red or pinkish bracts which trail down like ribbons as the new leaves unfold, for example in *R. thomsonii, R. habrotrichum* and *R. × loderi.* The leaves of many species, and a few hybrids, have an interesting indumentum. This is a covering, usually furry, that is often found all over the young shoots and remains on the underside of the adult leaf. It shows up to best advantage when the plant is tall enough to walk under. *R. falconeri* has a very handsome, bright brown indumentum, which contrasts spectacularly with the leatherly green upper leaf surface and the creamy yellow flowers. *R. fulvum* is another splendid foliage species whose leaves are not so large; this indumentum shows and vanishes as the leaves are rippled by the wind.

While several rhododendrons, such as *R. williamsianum* and *R. moupinense* have bronze new growth, there is one variety, as far as I know, that has coloured foliage. This is 'Elizabeth Lockhart', a sport of Humming Bird discovered by Professor Lockhart of Aberdeen. It has leaves rather similar in colour to those of a copper beech—it is described more fully in the section on hybrids.

The largest leaves in the genus are found in *R. sinogrande*, where in young plants they may be almost 3ft long, bright green above and silvery below. When the plant reaches flowering size, the new leaves are smaller. For this species, wind shelter must be very complete. In *R. hodgsonii*, the indumentum is like a shiny, metallic skin that covers the new growth and remains in patches on the upper sides of the adult leaves, making them look as if they were scattered with spots of mica.

There are quite a number of tallish species and hybrids which do not have large leaves and so are rather easier to grow. As their habit of growth is usually open, they are not bulky plants and would not look out of scale even in quite a small garden, where they are useful for adding a bit of height to a planting. *R. thomsonii* is one of the finest and is fairly hardy. Although the best and most commonly seen form has blood-red flowers, there are forms with wishy-washy pink flowers that should be avoided at all costs. This is more easily said than done, as a plant may not flower for several years after purchase, but if it is bought from a reputable firm, and a red form is specified, it should be all right. *R. thomsonii*

R. cinnabarinum is a lovely plant with elegant, long-tubed flowers and neat blue-green foliage. This is var. *roylei* 'Magnificum', with plum red flowers.

has blue-green oblong leaves, especially blue when they have just unfolded, and lovely smooth, cinnamon-coloured, peeling bark. It is worth mentioning here that rhododendrons with smooth bark take very badly to pruning. However, there should be no need to prune any rhododendron, as they almost always grow naturally in an attractive shape, unless forced out or up by another plant that is too close, and if they were properly chosen in the first place to fit the space available, should not grow too large.

The Triflorum series has a number of tallish, slender species. *R. yunnanense* is one of the best of all rhododendrons; it is very free-flowering, with white, lavender or pink flower, and can stand exposure. *R. augustinii* at its best is a superlative plant with luminous, violet-blue flowers, but these appear in April and so it should not be placed in a part of the garden particularly liable to frost. The colour of this species seems to vary both with the soil in which it grows and with the weather, as well as with the form of the plant. There is a splendid hybrid called 'Electra' which is very free-flowering, deep in colour and slightly later than *R. augustinii* itself, but it is possibly more tender. I suppose strictly speaking, it is not a hybrid but a selected form of the species, as the other parent was *R. chasmanthum* which has now lost specific rank and is regarded as a variety of *R. augustinii.*

R. cinnabarinum is another tallish but un-bulky species, with very distinctive long, tubular flowers and oblong, grey-green foliage. 'Lady Chamberlain' and 'Lady Rosebery' are first-class hybrids of it. They are similar in habit but have larger flowers, and need some shelter in most gardens.

Rhododendrons for the Centre of the Border

There are many good, hardy species and hybrids available of intermediate size, most of which have a neat, rounded habit that contrasts pleasantly with the tall varieties. *R. haematodes, R. wardii, R. campylocarpum, R. neriiflorum,* Fabia, Mayday, Elizabeth, Brocade and Tally-ho are just a few examples of what is available. Others are described in the chapters on species and hybrids. Types such as these can form the central part of a shrub border.

Deciduous azaleas fit in very well here. With these, it is as well to keep separate the species and the hybrids. The widely grown Mollis, Ghent and Knap Hill hybrids are mostly yellow, orange, salmon or red (largely derived from the American *R. calendulaceum* in their ancestry) while many of the most beautiful species, such as *R. albrechtii* and the ultra-hardy *R. schlippenbachii* (to $-25°F$), both Japanese species, have flowers that are on the blue side of pink, and these two colour ranges are not very happy together.

'Brocade' has the loose, graceful truss of bell-shaped pink flowers and rounded leaves typical of hybrids of *R. williamsianum*.

Dwarf Species for Front Planting

For the front of the beds, there are plenty of dwarf species, and some hybrids to choose from. Traditionally, these are grown in rock gardens, but these must be *real* rock gardens, with large boulders buried for about three-quarters of their bulk, and not 'rockeries'—Christmas pudding confections with small stones scattered over a mound of earth, fortunately less common now than in the past. But there is no need to construct a rock garden to grow dwarf rhododendrons, as these alpine forms are just as happy in a humus-filled border. Those that form dense clumps like *R. impeditum* and other members of the Lapponicum series; *R. pemakoense* and some of the evergreen azaleas, look particularly well. As with heathers, two or three plants together make a better effect than one on its own, and the plants seem happier, growing through and into each other.

FLOWERS TO GROW WITH RHODODENDRONS

A certain difficulty occurs here which is, to define the sort of plant that looks right with rhododendrons. Anyone who grows species and good hybrids will know the type of plant, but it is not easy to explain. For example, few people would grow dahlias or gladioli amongst rhododendrons, yet lilies look very much at home. Shrub roses fit in well, but not hybrid teas. Perhaps the answer is that any plant that is near the wild form and has a natural, informal appearance looks right, but not ones with long garden histories, that have been extensively bred and selected. Yet even this does not cover every case, as camellias have long been cultivated in Japan, and yet they associate perfectly with rhododendrons.

Even more important than the appearance of the complementary plants is their soil preferences—in other words, one wants plants that like a moist, well-drained acid soil with plenty of humus and not too sunny and exposed a situation. Trees are needed, both to give the necessary height and the desirable dappled shade, but forest trees are out of place in the small to medium, modern garden. A tree that has to be lopped because it has grown too big for its site never looks well. There are plenty of small, neat-growing trees that give not too dense a shade and are of a scale suitable for any but the smallest garden. Many of the ornamental cherries are of this type, such as Prunus 'Accolade' (*P. subhirtella* × *P. sargentii*) and other varieties *P. subhirtella*; *P. incisa*, the cut-leafed cherry; *P. serrulata* 'Tai Haku' with large, pendant white flowers and 'Ukon' with soft yellow blossoms. I am not giving long lists or detailed descriptions of these, as most nurseries have quite a varied stock of them, and also of flowering crabs, another tree of the right sort of size. 'John Downie' is a good variety, with attractive white blossom followed by edible red and yellow fruit in autumn.

There are a number of *Sorbus* species that are useful as they have fruit of various colours—unfortunately enjoyed by birds, although the white and pink varieties are reputedly less likely to be eaten. They usually give good autumn colour as well. *S. cashmiriana* has white fruit as big as marbles following pink flowers in spring, and ferny foliage, and is not likely to grow to more than 15ft. *S. hupehensis* grows to 20–30ft and has white fruit that turn pink. 'Joseph Rock' has yellow berries and *S. sargentiana* has orange-red fruit and particularly good autumn colour.

The really big tree magnolias, such as the lovely pink *M. campbellii* and *M. mollicomata*, are too large for most gardens, as they grow to 50ft or more, but some of the smaller ones are very suitable. I like *M. salicifolia* very much; it can reach 30ft but is usually less, and forms a graceful, small tree with willow-shaped leaves and starry white, precocious flowers. The bark, when scraped, smells like lemon verbena. *M. stellata* is very like it in flower, but forms a bush of 10–15ft. *M. kobus* also flowers early, in April, but has larger flowers and broader leaves and can form a 30ft tree. *M. sieboldii*, once called *M. parviflora*, makes a large bush or small tree, 10–15ft high. The flowers are scented, cup-shaped, white with a boss of red stamens; they start to open in May and go on, off and on, until August. The leaves are oblong, usually 4 or 5in long. *M. sinensis* and *M. wilsonii* are very much alike, with pendulous white flowers, again with red stamens, up to 5in across in May and June. *M.* × *soulangeana* is probably the magnolia most often seen; it forms a spreading small tree or large shrub with tulip-shaped white flowers stained with purple. Var. *lennei* has rose-purple flowers and var. *alba*, with pure white flowers is, I think, the most effective.

Acer palmatum atropurpureum, the red-leaved Japanese maple, casts quite a dense shade when in full leaf, but is a most attractive small tree; it is slow-growing, but can reach 20ft. It needs a fairly sheltered site, as the young leaves can be shrivelled by frost or cold winds. *A. palmatum* 'Ozakazuki' is an elegant little tree up to about 15ft, which turns a splendid red in autumn. Two other small trees with good autumn colour are *Amelanchier laevis*, which has clusters of starry white flowers in April and May and coppery young growth, and *Enkianthus campanulatus*, one of the relatively few trees in the Ericaceae. It has clusters of creamy bell-shaped flowers streaked with red, in May; it is not showy in flower but is pleasant and graceful. It grows from 10 to 15ft.

While lilacs and laburnums are too well known to need description, there are two genera from the southern hemisphere that are unfamiliar to most people, and are very well worth growing in mild areas. The genus Embothrium comes from Chile. *E. coccineum lanceolatum* 'Norquinco Valley' seems to be the hardiest form. It is a tree that likes the same sort of conditions as the larger rhododendrons. It is a most spectacular plant where it can be grown, with semi-evergreen lanceolate leaves and brilliant scarlet bottle-brush flowers in May. Once it has settled down, and this may take some time, it grows quickly and makes a narrow, 30ft tree.

Eucryphia glutinosa is another Chilean species. It is a small tree with pinnate leaves that turn orange-red in autumn and hang long on the tree. It has beautiful single white flowers about 3in in diameter in July and August, but unfortunately the display does not last for long. *E.* × *intermedia* (*E. glutinosa* × *E. lucida*) 'Rostrevor' is fast-growing and free-flowering, slightly later than the last species. *E.* × *nymansensis* (*E. glutinosa* × *E. cordifolia*) is evergreen and again has white flowers in August and September. All these like moist, lime-free soils and sheltered positions.

Cercis siliquastrum, the Judas tree, also needs a mild area, but likes full sun and good drainage. It is attractive and not very often seen, with rosy-purple pea flowers in May and heart-shaped leaves. It is supposed to be the tree from which Judas hanged himself.

Garden Layers

A garden can be thought of as having three layers—tree, shrub and ground. The tree layer, of course, is discontinuous; one does not want a complete canopy. Turning to the shrub layer, there is a need for late flowerers to balance the predominantly early rhododendrons (although there are some late species, such as the azalea *R. viscosum*, which blooms in August). The hydrangeas are predominant here, especially the lacecaps, which accord better with a naturalistic effect then do the large-headed hortensias. All of these (lacecaps and hortensias) are considered to be forms of the hybrid *H. × macrophylla*. There are many varieties which differ considerably in flowering time and hardiness. 'Bluewave' is one of the most easily obtainable and in an acid soil has really strong blue colouring. It makes a large bush about 5ft tall and as much across and is very hardy. It starts to flower in August. 'Whitewave' is similar, but of course, white, and is earlier. 'Lilacina' has blue flowers in an acid soil and the leaves have a distinctive brown edging. 'Grayswood' is a variety of *H. serrata* and also flowers in July and August. It is a striking plant whose flowers are white at first, then turn pink and finally crimson as the flowers age. It can grow to about 5ft. *H. quercifolia* is still taller, growing to about 6ft. It has panicles of creamy flowers and large leaves with scalloped edges. *H. villosa* has long, furry dark leaves and lacecap-style lavender flowers. It can grow to over 6ft, with a greater spread, but must have a sheltered site. Both of these flower in August and September.

Hardy fuchsias are also good for late colour, and hypericums and potentillas add yellow to the garden landscape from July on until autumn.

The slender, arching branches of the brooms make a good contrast with the more solid shapes of rhododendrons. They have a wide range of flowering times, from the pale creamy-yellow sprays of the April-flowering *Cytisus × praecox* to the vivid yellow pea-flowers of *Spartium junceum* from July on. *Genista aetnensis*, another late-flowering species, is even more useful as it makes a slender bush up to 15ft tall which casts the light shade that rhododendrons like, and is itself covered with pale yellow flowers. The pink and red and bicolour brooms are, I think, less effective, but one I like very much is the white Spanish broom, *Cytisus multiflorus*, which flowers in May with the deciduous azaleas. Ideally, brooms should have a light, dry soil, but in a sunny position they seem to be happy in a good rhododendron soil.

In spite of the Victorian reputation for tenderness that still clings to them, camellias are pretty hardy and should grow in most gardens that can grow rhododendrons. They are excellent companions for rhododendrons as they too like moist, shady conditions and the same sort of soil, although they are more tolerant of soils tending to neutrality. Most of the commonly grown camellias are cultivars of *C. japonica*. All have shiny, pointed, evergreen leaves, and can eventually form large bushes (not trees) of 6–10ft high. The flowers may be single, semi-double or double; white, pink, red or striped. The single and semi-double varieties usually have a handsome boss of yellow stamens in the centre. Most varieties flower from March to early May; there are so many that I can only mention a very few of the more readily available and reliable ones. 'Jupiter' is single, bright red with yellow stamens. 'Donckelarii' has red, semi-double flowers, usually striped with white. 'Lady Clare' is a large, opulent, semi-double pink. 'Magnoliiflora' has beautifully formed, pale pink, double or semi-double flowers. 'Tricolor' is white with crimson stripes. All these flower less well in northern areas, where, if they are grown, they should be given more direct sunlight.

The cultivars of C. × williamsii, a hybrid between C. japonica and C. saluensis, are even better for general garden use. I have found that these grow faster and flower younger and more profusely than the forms of C. japonica, even in areas where the latter are less successful. The best known is 'Donation', which has large, pink, semi-double flowers that start to open in January and last for several weeks, dropping neatly off the bush when they finish. I have seen the flowers encrusted with frost and remain undamaged, even in an east-facing position. 'J. C. Williams' is a single pink and 'Francis Hanger' a single white.

'Salutation' is a cross of C. reticulata and C. saluensis. It has pink, semi-double flowers in December and January. 'Cornish Snow' is another saluensis hybrid, this time with C. cuspidata. It is a distinctive plant, with small, white flowers with drooping petals borne along the branches.

C. reticulata, in its wild form which has large, single pink flowers, is fairly hardy, but the various cultivars of this species can only be grown outside in mild areas.

Most of the shrub roses take up a lot of space, but if that can be spared, some should be grown. Rosa Mundi, sometimes called Rosa gallica versicolor is one of the more compact varieties, rarely growing to more than 4ft × 4, and it does not mind being clipped. It is an unusual looking plant with semi-double pink flowers striped and blotched with purple. Two other Gallica roses, both of which could be expected to grow to about 5 × 4, are Charles de Mills with deep wine crimson flowers and Cardinal de Richlieu, which is deep purple. It is reputed to dislike hot, dry soils, but this is not likely to be a problem in a garden that grows rhododendrons.

Rosa rubrifolia has unspectacular single pink flowers; it is grown for its foliage which has an indescribable purplish sheen, not at all like the purplish brown foliage of plants like *Prunus cerasifera* 'Pissardii'.

A few others that I like particularly include 'Nevada', which is definitely large and vigorous, it can reach 8ft high and more across, but at the end of May and in early June it is absolutely smothered in large, white single flowers with a yellow boss of stamens. It produces flowers in much less profusion on through the summer. 'Marguerite Hilling' is a pink version that to my mind is much less attractive. 'Canary Bird' is one of the earliest roses to flower, in May, with bright yellow single flowers. 'Frühlingsgold' is only slightly later and has paler, larger flowers and graceful arching branches. Both of these grow to about 7ft × 7. Any specialist catalogue will list many more, and should give the expected size.

Some of the floribundas fit in quite well, especially if they are pruned only lightly. One of the best is Iceberg, whose white flowers are a good foil for bright colours.

While on the subject of roses, climbers should not be forgotten. It is surprising how often one sees vertical space wasted in a garden. Any wall or fence can be used to support a climbing rose, which can itself in turn offer support to a clematis.

Pieris is an evergreen genus of the Ericaceae that has very much the same soil and climatic preferences as rhododendrons. *P. formosa forrestii* is by a long way the most striking species, as its new growth is a brilliant scarlet, more vivid than most flowers, but it needs a sheltered spot in mild areas as that new growth can appear very early; it is a plant that seems to have little sense of time: any precociously early spell will lure it on, and then it gets frosted. All of the Pierises have hanging racemes of creamy flowers like lily-of-the-valley.

The Ground Layer

There are many suitable candidates here. It is important to achieve contrasts of leaf shape. The large leaves of hostas, bergenias and the spotted pulmonarias show off to good advantage the small, leathery ones of the dwarf rhododendrons, and the spiky foliage of irises adds interest. Heathers are so well known as associates of rhododendrons that there is no need to go further into them here. In thick shade, ferns and bluebells look well.

Trilliums are attractive plants that look well in shady places, and look unusual with three large, white or reddish petals, and three leaves encircling the stem. There are a number of species, all basically similar.

Two genera that seem to blend particularly well with rhododendrons are *Primula* and *Meconopsis*. The native Welsh Poppy, *M. cambrica*, grows and seeds itself like a weed, but is nevertheless useful with its light green, ferny leaves and cheerful yellow flowers that keep on appearing from early spring until autumn. There is an orange form, but it is much less effective. After this, the most commonly seen member of the genus is *M. betonicifolia* (once known as *M. baileyi*), the blue Himalayan poppy. This is a lovely plant which enjoys the same sort of humus soil and semi-shade as do rhododendrons, and should persist for years in the garden, seeding itself if conditions are right. It is in flower at the same time as the geranium red *R. griersonianum* and the two colours make a pleasant combination. There are a number of other species of meconopsis that are well worth trying, although they may not be easy to obtain. It is usually possible to get seed through the seed exchange schemes run by the Alpine Garden Society and the Scottish Rock Garden Club. *M. regia* is monocarpic, that is it differs from an annual in that its life-cycle is not over in one year, but like an annual, it dies after flowering. Fortunately, plants grown from the same sowing will not all flower in the same year, and so, if seed is collected, it is not too difficult to keep a succession going. *M. dwojii*, yellow with hairs coming from black dots on the leaves like a tabby-cat's whiskers; *M. quintuplinervia*, the 'harebell poppy' with pendant, lavender flowers; *M. horridula*, a very variable species with flowers of different shades of blue and lavender, and one of the easiest to grow in the south of England; *M. nepaulensis* with yellow, pink or red flowers and *M. latifolia*, the yellow 'lampshade poppy', are all worth attempting. Some of the species, notably *M. nepaulensis* and *M. regia* have beautiful rosettes of furry leaves that persist for two or three years until the plant flowers. *M. grandis* has the largest flowers in the genus, of a lovely deep blue colour.

With primulas, there is much more choice. Most of the European species are rock garden plants, but many of the Asiatics do well in shrub beds, particularly the candelabra species, which are often robust and long-lived. These have flowers in successive whorls up a stem that elongates as fresh circles of flowers open, and may eventually be 2ft tall or even more. *P. pulverulenta* has crimson flowers, and the stem and buds are covered with a white, mealy farina. There are hybrid forms such as 'Inverewe' or 'Bartley's Strain' which have flowers in various shades of pink, salmon and apricot. This species, like most of the candelabras, likes a moist, shaded situation, and given that, should persist for years and seed itself copiously. *P. japonica* is rather similar, but is coarser and lacks farina. It is, however, more adaptable as to situation, growing so prolifically as to be almost a weed. We have it coming up in cracks in a stone path. *P. helodoxa* is 2ft tall and yellow; *P. bulleyana* is on a smaller scale and has deeper yellow flowers opening from reddish-orange buds. This last species dies down completely below ground in winter. Even smaller is *P. cockburniana*, with burnt-orange flowers, but unfortunately it seems to be short-lived, like two other outstanding species not of the candelabra type, *P. nutans*, which has luminous violet bells powdered with white at the base, and *P. vialii*, with spikes of lilac flowers opening from red bracts. *P. chionantha* is a useful, early-flowering species with smooth, light-green leaves, heavily powdered stems and umbels of white or mauve flowers. *P. denticulata* is the well-known Easter-flowering drumstick primula, with round heads of lilac flowers. This is easy and reliable but the leaves grow very large after flowering, so clumps must be sited where they will not be too much in the way. This species has various selected colour forms in white, deep purple and reddish purple that tend to be less vigorous. It has an attractive late flowering relative in *P. capitata*, which is altogether on a smaller scale, with purple flowers well set off by heavily powdered buds. It starts flowering about the end of July and goes on until September or October. *P. florindae* and *P. alpicola* both look rather like very large cowslips. Both are yellow in the commonest forms, but the former has a copper-coloured variety, and the latter has a white form (var. *alba*) and a violet form (var. *violaceae*). These are fairly easy in damp situations.

Both primulas and meconopsis are happier in areas where there is not too much winter damp as this rots the crown when the plant is not growing and, like rhododendrons, they do not really like hot, dry summers. In the British Isles, they are in general happier in the north than in the south.

Bulbs

Many bulbous plants go well with rhododendrons, the spring flowering ones with deciduous azaleas in particular. Again, the more formal types seem less suitable. Large-headed daffodils look less 'right' than some of the smaller species and hybrids, such as the native Lent-lily, *Narcissus pseudonarcissus*; 'Thalia', a *N. triandrus* hybrid with clusters of pure white flowers, and 'Peeping Tom', a *N. cyclamineus* hybrid. The miniature species such as *N. bulbocodium* and *N. cyclamineus* tend to get lost in a shrub border. Tulips are too stiff and in any case like very different cultural conditions, as they thrive on summer baking. *Crocus* species, scillas, chionodoxas and pushkinias are all gay and take up little space. Their main enemy in a garden seems to be mice.

Lilies mix very well with rhododendrons, as most of them also like a well-drained, peaty soil. The shrubs give the necessary shade at the roots and the long-stemmed flowers come up through the branches into the sunlight. *L. regale, L. speciosum* and various hybrids seem happy like this. Another summer-flowering bulbous plant I like is *Galtonia candicans*, which resembles a large, white bluebell and persists well from year to year.

The Madeira orchid, *Dactylorhiza foliosa*, is tuberous-rooted, not bulbous. I have rarely seen it in other gardens, and have never seen it offered in a catalogue, but I have grown it easily in different parts of Britain, and it multiplies rapidly. It has fat spikes of royal purple flowers a foot or more tall coming from dense clumps of slightly fleshy leaves. It dies back in winter, but you can see the next year's buds just below the soil surface. It would be easy to protect these in a very cold climate, but I have so far found it completely hardy. It flowers in June.

Agapanthus, the splendid blue African lily, flowers in August. There are hardy varieties available, and in cold areas they can be covered with straw or bracken in winter. The plants we grow came from seed collected in Kenya and are now in their ninth year, having survived some hard frosts outside without protection.

Many herbaceous perennials will blend in with the sort of planting scheme I have been describing. The thing to keep in mind when selecting plants from a catalogue is their soil preferences; if they are described as liking a dry sunny position with poor soil, they must be avoided. Astilbes and rodgersias are the sort of plant that should be tried.

Colour Schemes

I said something about colour schemes at the beginning of the chapter. Plant colour-schemes are not easy to work out because the timing has to be so exact and in any one season, the flowering time of some plants may be advanced or retarded, but not that of others. The most successful combinations in our gardens seem to have come about accidentally. *R. neriiflorum* is usually in flower at the same time as grape hyacinths; when we noticed that, we planted some under and around the neriiflorum as the soft blue and red blend so well. *R. luteum*, the common sweet-scented, yellow Pontic azalea and the white Spanish broom, *Cytisus multiflorus*, flower together. In one garden, bushes of these were planted in front of a red-leaved Japanese maple which was in bright new leaf at just the right time, and this is another combination we always try to repeat, although in our present garden we will have a long wait as the original maple was a wide, spreading tree about 20ft tall. *R. griersonianum*, *Meconopsis betonicifolia* and *Dactylorhiza foliosa* more vivid of geranium red, sky blue and rich purple—and give much pleasure. The violet blues of many rhododendrons, such as Blue Diamond and other *R. augustinii* hybrids, blend pleasantly with soft yellows—not the hard, bright gold of daffodils but the pale tint of primroses and some of the yellow dwarfs such as *R. sargentianum*, *R. hanceanum nanum*, Chikor and Chink.

If deciduous azaleas are being grown in a mass, for example in light woodland, where they look so well, it seems to be important to include a fairly large proportion of yellow and cream varieties. This sets off the brighter salmons and reds and binds the colours together, as it were.

Certain colours are notoriously difficult to place. One that comes to mind is the strident magenta of the rhododendron 'Cynthia', one of the oldest and commonest hardy hybrids. Many people must have bought a house with a plant of this flourishing in the garden. The only colours that can survive with this are a soft buff-yellow, like rhododendron 'Letty Edwards', which is usually in flower at the same time, or better still, green. I know two massive bushes—if they can be called that as they must be a good 30ft tall—growing amongst the forest trees lining a bypass. In the midst of woodland they would look garish and out of place, but beside the road, which is itself artificial, surrounded by an ocean of green, they have an admirable barbaric splendour.

CHAPTER 5

Propagation

Rhododendrons can be propagated by any of the standard methods—seed, cuttings, layering or grafting. The last of these, grafting, I shall not deal with, as rhododendrons and azaleas are much better grown on their own roots.

Growing rhododendrons from seed is very easy. Admittedly, one needs patience, but sometimes less than one might think, as quite a number of dwarfs will flower in three or four years from sowing, and with the larger species, almost equal satisfaction is to be gained from watching them grow. Whether seed comes true or not, depends on where and when it was collected. If the plant from which the seed was taken was the only rhododendron near which was in flower at a particular time, then the odds are very much in favour of the seed coming true. If, however, the plant is surrounded by related species, all in flower together, then you are likely to raise a batch of hybrids. One can, of course, self-pollinate flowers, and then be certain of getting the true species. I do not think the risk of hybridization is quite as great as it is sometimes made out to be, because of the differences in flowering time—after all, virtually all the species in cultivation were grown from seed collected in the wild, and while a few are of suspect validity, the majority come true.

When should seed be collected? The time usually recommended is in autumn, say about October. The pod, which may not be completely brown and dry, is put in an envelope and left in a warm (but not too hot) room and will probably open of its own accord as it dries out. The seeds can be sown around January or February and usually germinate in two to four weeks. I have always had the best results, however, from seeds collected in early spring, when the pods are just starting to open naturally—depending on the weather, this can be from mid March to early May. Even if the pods seem fully open and most of the seed seems to have gone, there will usually be plenty left at the bottom of the pod. Rhododendrons produce prodigious quantities of small, light seed. Seed collected like this and sown immediately almost always germinates en masse in a very short time; a fortnight on average, but sometimes as little as a week, and the seedlings grow away very quickly.

Seed can be sown in a number of media. Fine peat alone can be used, but it cakes on drying and is difficult to rewet. Unless the pans can be sprayed daily, a peat/sand/chalk-free loam mixture is easier. Well-rotted pine needles are good, but one must be careful that there are no feral *R. ponticum* bushes around, or one may find that the seedlings nurtured for years are just that. Sphagnum moss is excellent, either alone or mixed with loam. It should be dried in the sun and then can be rubbed or sieved to a fairly fine consistency; not too fine or the structure, which is one of the great assets of this medium, as it is well-aerated yet retentive of water, is destroyed. I have gone over almost entirely to using sphagnum for growing rhododendron seedlings. It is supposed to be sterile, but I find that moss and algae do grow on it although less prolifically than on other media. It also appears to contain some growth-promoting substance. I have done no detailed trials on this, but simply from observation, I would say that seedlings growing in a medium containing sphagnum, and also in pure sphagnum (which was found less successful than mixed composts in the paper referred to) grow much more rapidly and vigorously than those in any other medium.

Whatever the medium used, the seeds should be scattered on the surface and the pots should be either placed in a cold frame or a polythene bag on a windowsill in the house. This sealing up with either glass or polythene is essential, as the seeds must not be allowed to dry out. Any of the media mentioned can be sterilized by putting it in an oven (before the seeds are sown, of course) at about 200°F for about half an hour. The temperature must not be so high as to burn up the organic matter. Pots should be well scrubbed and any pieces of pod or chaff mixed with the seeds should be removed, as such foreign bodies are a fertile source of fungi. Sterilization is not essential, but it is advisable as a dense growth of moss or algae can smother small seedlings. The seedlings can be pricked out when they are big enough to handle, which is usually when they have a couple of pairs of true leaves. On the other hand, if they are growing on well and are not too dense, they can be left alone until the following year.

Once the true leaves have appeared, the polythene can be removed, as this slows down the growth of moss and algae, if there are any there. I keep seedlings indoors for the first winter, then plunge the pots outside for the summer. The following winter, the pots are either left out or are taken in again, depending on the size and vigour of the seedlings and the hardiness of the species. The next summer, they can be planted out. It is not worth taking chances with seedlings of doubtful hardiness, as many plants that are hardy when large, are susceptible to frost when young.

Seedlings may be several years old before they develop certain characteristics of the species, such as indumentum. Often the underside of the leaves is a dark, purplish red, due to the presence of an anthocyanin pigment—I have noticed this in a number of species, particularly R. *dichroanthum* in its first year. The colour fades as the seedlings grow. Sometimes the leaves turn green before hairs appear and sometimes hairs grow while the undersurface is still red. Professor Bayley Balfour did a study on this and described the method of transition for various species. In R. *fictolacteum*, for example, the undersurface remains red and glandular until the third year and then the characteristic buff indumentum develops, while in R. *bullatum* the undersurface is not completely hairy until the sixth year. Knowing this eliminates one source of worry, when the leaves of seedlings do not seem at all like those of the adult of the species they are supposed to be. The leaves should be more or less the adult *shape* by the end of the second year.

While it is possible to make most kinds of rhododendron stike from cuttings, the large-leaved species and most of the elepidotes (with the notable exception of the evergreen azaleas) are difficult. One often reads that the smaller the leaf, the later in the season the cuttings should be taken; a good general rule for most cuttings is to take them when the current season's growth is just starting to harden off. Short side shoots with a heel seem to be best; the ends can be dipped in a hormone rooting powder (I am never sure how much good this does, but it certainly does no harm, and it is best to be on the safe side). The cuttings should be placed in a peat/sand mixture and must be kept enclosed in a frame, or a pot in a polythene bag if there are only a few, or a wooden box with a close-fitting glass top. Small-leaved varieties will often strike if the box or pot is plunged in a shady part of the garden, but the larger the leaf, the more necessary it is to provide bottom heat. If a mist-propagating unit is available, this, of course, will give much quicker and more certain results.

For the gardener who merely wants to increase his own favourite plants and perhaps have one spare for a friend, layering is one of the best methods. For this, a *young* branch is bent down so that a portion near the tip can be buried underground. This usually needs to be anchored with some kind of peg—one cut from a forked twig will do—so that there is a fairly abrupt bend where the uncovered twig grows upwards. A flat stone placed on top of the soil so that it covers the bend helps to keep everything in place and also to keep conditions moist, which encourages rooting. The layered branch can then be left alone for about a year, and can then be cut off and removed, if a preliminary excavation shows that roots have formed. If the branch is layered into a wooden box, the layer can be removed with no disturbance to the roots.

Many plants which one would wish to layer do not have any branches conveniently sited for ground layering. With these, air-layering can be tried. In spring, a branch of the previous year's growth is slit for 1–2 in along its length, making the cut about halfway through. The faces of the cut should have a hormone powder dusted on; there seems to be fairly general agreement that in air-layering, this is essential. Then damp (but not soggy) sphagnum is tied around the slit and the whole is wound round with polythene, whose ends should be sealed to the branch with insulating tape so that moisture is kept both in and out. All going well, by the following year, roots should be visible through the polythene, and the branch can be detached. These are 'water roots' however, and there is still likely to be some difficulty in establishing them in soil. Once the branch has been cut off, it should be potted up in a very open and light peat/loam/sand mixture, and should be kept enclosed for some time in a frame before it is gradually hardened off. This method is normally used only for the larger species and hybrids, that are more difficult to propagate by cuttings, and that have branches of a reasonable thickness.

CHAPTER 6

Pests and Diseases

Rhododendrons are cursed with fewer blights and banes than most plants, but there are still a few that might trouble the grower. They can be considered in two categories—those that are specific to rhododendrons, and those that can attack any plant.

In the former group, I suppose the most serious must be Bud Blast, which is particularly prevalent in the south of England. It is found in other places; in the United States it is only common on the native species *R. macrophyllum*. The disease is caused by the combination of a fungus, *Pycnostysanus azaleae*, and an insect, the Rhododendron Leafhopper, *Graphocephala coccinea*. The adults of the latter are about $\frac{1}{2}$in long, and are gaily patterned in red and green. They lay eggs under the epidermis of the bud scales; these hatch in early May and the hoppers become adult at the end of July. In themselves they do little damage, but the wounds may be entered by the spores of the fungus. The buds start to turn brown or greyish in September, and in spring they are covered with what looks like black hairs about 1mm long, with a knob on the end of each. These are the fruiting bodies of the fungus; infected buds should be picked off and burnt,

Bud Blast

together with about 2 in of the diseased shoot. So far, there is no effective spray against the fungus, so the best protection is to spray the insects with malathion in August and September. I am not giving specific dosages of any fungicides or insecticides mentioned, as instructions are given on the packets of the various proprietary brands.

Rhododendron Bug, *Stephanitis rhododendri*, is now quite widespread in the south of England. It was introduced from the United States around 1910. The upper surfaces of the leaves become mottled yellow and the lower develop brownish spots. Some species and hybrids are more vulnerable to attack than others, *R. catawbiense* and its progeny (which includes quite a number of the 'hardy hybrids') being particularly susceptible. The adult bugs are sun-loving, so that plants in deep shade are rarely affected. The bugs are about 4mm long, dark brown, and lay eggs on the undersides of the leaves in summer and autumn, and the young bugs feed from the following May. Light attacks can be cured by picking off infested leaves and squashing the bugs. Gamma-BNC and malathion can be used as sprays in May and June, but it is important to be sure that the undersides of the leaves, where the colonies feed, are properly wetted.

Rhododendron Whitefly, *Dialeurodes chittendeni*, is a pest of certain species and hybrids, again mostly in southern England—the unfortunate region where pests are concerned. Signs of attack are rather similar to the last mentioned, but there is no spottiness on the undersides of the leaves. Smooth-leaved species and hybrids are prone to attack and it is worth examining the leaves of any plants brought into the garden. Infected leaves should be removed and burnt. The small, white adults swarm under the upper leaves in June and July and lay eggs there which hatch into scale-like nymphs. Both stages suck the sap, and honeydew is produced which falls on to lower leaves and provides a medium for the growth of sooty moulds. The undersides of the leaves should be sprayed two or three times at fortnightly intervals with malathion.

The Azalea Whitefly, *Aleyrodes azaleae*, is a similar insect that if found in the eastern United States, where it attacks evergreen azaleas, particularly *R. mucronatum* and related species and their hybrids. Kurumes do not seem to be affected. The control is the same as for the previous species.

Until recently, aphids have not been a pest of rhododendrons, except in greenhouses and on some deciduous azaleas. However, in 1971, *Masonaphis lambersi*, a species native to the

United States, was found on rhododendrons in southern England and Holland. Young growing shoots were attacked and became distorted. Insects have so far been definitely recorded on Doncaster and Mrs G. W. Leak and on *R. ponticum*, as well as on an unnamed deciduous azalea and on numerous evergreen hybrids. Some of the infestations have been heavy, and it is to be hoped that this is not going to become a permanent fact of life, although it seems sadly probable that it will.

All the insects mentioned may be controlled by insecticides such as malathion, which is a contact insecticide, that is, it works only when the spray lands on an insect or it walks on deposited droplets. This means that coverage of the plant has to be just about perfect. Rhododendron whitefly spread to the Pacific coast area of the United States and Canada about 40 years ago, but is not a serious problem there.

Systemic insecticides, which are carried around a plant in the sap, are much more effective and more easily applied. I understand that recommendations on their use may be forthcoming; in the meantime we have plucked up courage and sprayed our plants with 'Rogor' and harm has been done only to the pests.

Several kinds of fungi can affect rhododendrons. Two species cause spots on the leaves—one brown spots with white centres and the other, white spots with raised reddish margins. Neither is particularly serious and they can be controlled by picking off affected leaves.

Gall is caused by *Exobasidium vaccinii*. The galls are swollen, reddish lumps that may be formed on leaves, flowers or stems and should be picked off before they turn white, as this is a sign that the spores are being released. Evergreen azaleas, especially under glass, are most liable to be affected, and it can occur on other small-leaved rhododendrons. The plants can be sprayed with Bordeaux mixture or Zineb.

Chrysomyxa rhododendri is a not very common rust that causes brown and yellow suppurating spots under the leaves. Its alternate host is spruce, *Picea abies*, and while the fungus could be sprayed with any general fungicide such as zineb, if there are spruces about, there is certain to be reinfection.

This species is found in California, Oregon, Washington and British Columbia, within a couple of miles of the coast. *C. piperiana*, also with spruce as an alternate host, attacks *R. macrophyllum* in these western states. In the eastern United States, certain evergreen azaleas and rhododendrons, particularly *R. ponticum*, have been attacked by another rust, *Pucciniastrum myrtilli*, whose alternate host is hemlock (*Tsuga* spp.), although sometimes the fungus seems able to reinfect directly. However, none of these are very widespread or serious.

Of diseases not confined to rhododendrons, the most serious is Honey Fungus, *Armillaria mellea*. The affected plant just starts to die, without any other obvious symptoms, but if the bark is removed below ground level, the spreading white mycelium of the fungus can be seen, and in the ground, the characteristic black bootlaces called rhizomorphs. With this fungus, prevention is easier than cure. All dead stumps should be removed, whether they seem infected or not, and any infected roots should be destroyed. The fruiting bodies, yellowish toadstools, appear in late summer around the stump, in lines following the track of a root. The spores do not attack living trees but just dead wood. The rhizomorphs, however, affect the quick and the dead alike, although there are some grounds for believing that healthy plants, growing vigorously, are not attacked. Certainly attack is most likely on wet, heavy ground, so good drainage is helpful. If the infection has been confined to a small area, the ground can be sterilized by watering with a solution of 1 pint of formaldehyde to 6 gal of water.

Crown Gall, *Bacterium tumefaciens*, again is not confined to rhododendrons. It is an irregular, roundish swelling, soft and white when young, hard and brown when old, which can become bigger than a tennis ball. The disease is most prevalent on a wet soil and it is possible that infection can only occur through a wound. In a garden where this disease is known to be present, roots should be dipped in a fungicide before planting.

Sooty moulds are a group of fungi which grow on the honeydew secreted by aphids and whitefly. They are superficial but look nasty and cut out a certain amount of light to the leaves. Sooty mould can be a problem if plants are growing where they are overhung by trees that are prone to aphid attack, such as limes or sycamores.

Root Rot, or Rhododendron Wilt, *Phytophthora cinnamomi* is a very serious disease in parts of the United States, particularly warmer areas. It seems worse in heavy soils and where drainage is poor. *R. ponticum* seems to be very susceptible, and so grafted plants often suffer. *R. griersonianum* is also liable to infection. Infected plants wilt when others are fresh, and under the bark near ground level the tissue is brown and dead. Affected plants should be burnt and the soil treated with a fungicide such as Dithane D-14 (Nabam). This can be toxic if applied to foliage, but is believed to have a systemic effect on some Phytophthora spp.

In Rhododendron Blight, *Phytophthora cactorum*, another disease prevalent in America, the leaves curl up and whole branches die back. Such branches should be cut off well below the affected area and burnt. The disease is found usually on plants in dense shade, and like the last disease, is more of a problem in warm areas such as the southern states.

Various kinds of weevils, such as vine weevils, *Otiorhynchus sulcatus* and clay-coloured weevils, *O. singularis*, may attack foliage. They eat neat, circular patches from the edges of the leaves. They feed by night, and tend to hide under litter such as dead leaves during the day. Vine weevil leaf damage can be seen in the photograph of *R. rex*. The larvae feed on roots and can be serious pests in the United States, both on the Pacific Coast and in the east. The easiest method of control is to spray the adults on the plants with BHC, but the larvae can also be attacked by sprinkling BHC powder on the soil.

Occasionally rhododendron leaves are attacked by certain caterpillars, such as those of the Tortrix moth. These can be picked off by hand or sprayed with malathion or trichlorphon. I have never had rhododendron seedlings eaten by slugs, but I do not grow them in open ground. I would imagine that slugs would not invariably ignore them, particularly if nothing better was available. The main slug baits are based on metaldehyde and methiocarb. The latter is preferable, as it kills the slugs outright, while metaldehyde just paralyses them, and in cool, damp weather, they may recover.

I have not dealt with greenhouse pests, as they are not likely to concern readers of this book, and if they do, information could be found in a book on greenhouse culture. The names of pesticides and fungicides that I have mentioned will not be those by which various preparations are sold, as different firms have their own trade names, but the actual name of the compound has to be given somewhere on the packet.

Pests are not all as small as insects and fungi. Rabbits are troublesome in some places and seem to have a preference for dwarfs, which I suppose are more accessible. Grey squirrels can cause a problem and, while all will damage trees, certain individuals apparently develop a particular taste for rhododendrons. I have been told of one which persistently bit off, but did not eat, flowerbuds of *R. thomsonii* and chewed up the growth buds of Penjerrick. The same source records sporadic attacks on flower buds of various kinds over a period of years; attacks on growth buds are apparently rarer.

The only answer seems to be to shoot the offending individuals.

This longish list of pests may seem alarming, but attacks are not nearly so inevitable as, say, attacks of aphis and black spot on roses. In fact, the only rhododendron pest I have, so far, ever suffered from in a number of gardens, is vine weevil, and that to a very minor extent. It is probably possible to grow rhododendrons for a lifetime without meeting any of them. Ailing rhododendrons are much more likely to be suffering from some nutritional trouble caused by unsuitable soil or site than from an actual plant disease.

CHAPTER 7

Azaleas

Although rhododendrons and azaleas are now one and the same genus, there comes a point where azaleas must be dealt with separately, partly because their garden history has been so distinct from that of other rhododendrons. Most azaleas one sees in gardens are hybrids, and there are two main groups, the deciduous and the evergreens. Some of the deciduous azalea species were amongst the earliest rhododendrons to be brought into cultivation in Europe and the United States, most of them American natives such as *R. viscosum* and *R. nudiflorum* (discovered by John Bannister in Virginia in 1690).

The ancestry of some of the groups of hybrids is difficult to unravel, not less so because of the confusion over names that has occurred. The plant now known as *R. japonicum* used to be called *R. molle* and *Azalea mollis*. It is a deciduous species of the Luteum subseries, not at all like the evergreen 'Japanese azaleas' as might be suggested by its name. To add to the confusion, another closely related species is now called *R. molle*—in the past, it was known as *R. sinense*. The Mollis hybrids, possibly the most widely grown of all, are the result of crosses between various forms of these two species (*R.*

91

japonicum and *R. molle*), indeed some may just be forms of *R. japonicum*. In the 1870s, Louis van Houtte in Ghent was selecting and naming forms of the latter, and others in Holland and Belgium were crossing the two species. The yellow Anthony Koster and the orange Hugo Koster, which are still commercially available, date back to the end of the nineteenth century—the former received a FCC in 1893.

The Mollis hybrids are hardy, they grow 5 or 6ft tall and flower in May just before the leaves appear. The colours range from cream through yellow, salmon, pink, orange to red, but they rarely have any scent. There are a few double varieties, such as the yellow Phoebe.

The Ghent hybrids are generally a couple of weeks later in flowering than the Mollises and are even hardier. The colours are more muted and the flowers are elegant and long tubed, smaller individually than those of the Mollis hybrids, but with a heavy, honeysuckle perfume that can fill a garden. They were produced by complex interbreeding within the Luteum subseries. P. Mortier, a Ghent baker, started crossing the American species *R. calendulaceum* and *R. nudiflorum* in the 1820s and he passed on his seedlings to another breeder in Ghent. *R. viscosum* and *R. luteum* were added to the mix. Coccinea Speciosa, a bright orange-red that received an Award of Garden Merit from the RHS as recently as 1968, and Gloria Mundi, an orange with a yellow lobe, are two varieties that date from early days. There are some double Ghents, such as the still popular Narcissi flora.

The Rustica Flore Pleno hybrids are all double and are probably derived from double Ghents crossed with Mollis hybrids. They were developed in Belgium at the end of the nineteenth century.

The Occidentale hybrids were developed early this century by crossing the fragrant *R. occidentale* with Mollis hybrids. They flower one or two weeks later than the Ghents and like them, are sweetly scented and grow 6–8ft tall. The individual flowers are larger than those of the Ghents and are usually pink or white, with a yellow blotch.

The Knap Hill and Exbury hybrids have been bred and selected from all the preceding groups. Probably some also have *R. arborescens*, another American species, in their parentage. The flowers are 2 or 3in across, wide and flat with a long, slender tube, and there may be as many as 30 in one cluster. Many are scented and they have an exceptionally wide colour range, just about every shade that can be found in a deciduous azalea. A list of varieties and their colours is given at the end of the book.

The leaves of these deciduous azaleas often turn a rich red before they fall in autumn, which is a pleasant bonus, as they are well worth growing for their flowers alone. They are often grown in light woodland, and can be seen thus in many famous gardens, but this is not essential. In the sunlight, the flowers fade more quickly, but the plants will be more compact and floriferous. Although most make large bushes in time, they are not bulky-looking plants and do not look out of place in a small garden. It is always best to buy these plants on their own roots. Sometimes they are sold grafted on to *R. luteum* stock, but a strongly growing azalea will throw up suckers from the roots and in time the stock will overwhelm the scion. If one wants azaleas en masse and is not too fussy about the exact colours, un-named seedlings are very much cheaper than named varieties and usually turn out well.

The other type of azalea is the evergreen, often called Japanese azalea. These are not evergreen in the usual sense of the word. They have dimorphic leaves, that is, of two kinds. The spring leaves appear at, or just after, flowering, scattered along the branches. They fall in autumn, often turning yellow before they do so. The summer leaves unfold in early summer and are thicker, more leathery, smaller and darker than the spring leaves and are crowded at the ends of the branches. They are usually shed the following spring, but in some species, such as *R. indicum*, they may last for up to three years. The leaves often turn reddish during winter, and if the weather is really cold, most of them are shed.

Apart from *R. tashiroi*, a species not in general cultivation which has a subseries to itself, all evergreen azaleas are in the Obtusum subseries and all are Asiatic. This subseries contains 40 species, by the current RHS Handbook, and of these, 24 are listed as not being in cultivation. Probably about half of the remainder have been extensively used in hybridization. There are no yellows or oranges in the Obtusum subseries, but white, mauve, pink, red, purple and magenta. Some evergreen azaleas, such as *R. mucronatum* and *R. linearifolium*, which are doubtfully true species, have been cultivated in Japan for over 300 years.

The best known group of evergreen azaleas is the Kurumes, which were first seen in the west when a Japanese nurseryman, Kojiro Akashi of Kurume on the island of Kyushu, sent an exhibit to an 'Exposition' in San Francisco in 1915. In 1918, the plant collector E. H. Wilson visited Kurume and selected what he considered to be the best 50 forms for the Arnold Arboretum in Boston, Massachusetts. From there, a selection was sent to Wisley Gardens, Woking. Some proved not to be hardy, but many are still to be seen there, and in the Savill Garden in Windsor Great Park.

The kurumes are thought not to be hybrids, but selected forms of the wild *R. kiusianum*. Some people, however, believe that there is so much diversity in the kurumes that it is unlikely that they have arisen from one species, and consider that three species were involved in their development, namely *R. kiusianum*, *R. kaempferi* and *R. obtusum*, all of which are found

Evergreen azaleas at Wisley. These delightful and accommodating plants produce a blaze of colour year after year.

wild on Kyushu. The first two form natural hybrids wherever their ranges meet.

Evergreen azaleas should be grown in full exposure, to ensure a compact habit, and for the sun to ripen and harden off the wood and promote flowering. This is particularly important for the kurumes, which have been known to succumb to frost if not fully hardened. The kurumes are medium-growing, reaching 3 or 4ft eventually, with a beautifully symmetrical, tiered habit. Unfortunately the stems are rather brittle and are highly vulnerable to dogs and balls. They are fairly slow-growing. The flowers are smallish, $\frac{1}{2}$–$1\frac{1}{2}$in in diameter, but a plant in bloom is usually absolutely smothered. They are single, with some varieties hose-in-hose.

This is a phrase that needs some explanation. A hose-in-hose flower has a petaloid calyx, so that there appears to be two whorls of petals, one inside the other. This is not to be confused with a double flower, where the stamens are petaloid, so that the extra parts are all inside the true petals. In a semi-double flower, only some or part of the stamens have become transformed. Technically, double and semi-double flowers can also be hose-in-hose. A single, hose-in-hose flower is very attractive.

A group of large flowered hybrids flowers in May and June, after the kurumes. These are the Malvatica or Kaempferi

Kirin (hose-in-hose kurume azalea)

hybrids. 'Malvatica' is a hybrid of unknown parentage, found in a group of kurumes by Koster of Boskoop in Holland. He crossed it with the variable and hardy *R. kaempferi* and produced these hybrids which are hardier, taller and with larger flowers than the kurumes. The flowers are $1\frac{1}{2}$–$2\frac{1}{2}$in across in all the colours found in the Obtusum subseries. Fedora is deep pink, John Cairns is brick red and Naomi is salmon pink. Unfortunately the flowers tend to fade in strong sunlight, but apart from that, the plants, like the kurumes, do better in full exposure. In the south of England, the United States and New Zealand, it is best to place them where they will get some shade at least in the middle of the day.

The Vuyk hybrids are rather similar to the Kaempferis; Kaempferi and Mollis hybrids were involved in their breeding, and possibly *R. mucronatum* and *R. pulchrum* var. *maxwellii* as well. The aim was to produce hardy plants with large flowers. There are a number of varieties called after composers, of which I think Palestrina is outstanding, a vigorous plant with pure white flowers and bright green foliage. The names of Vuyk's Rosy Red and Vuyk's Scarlet are self-explanatory.

A good deal of work is currently being done in the United States on hybridizing evergreen azaleas. Two groups which have involved extensive breeding programmes are the Gable and Glenn Dale hybrids. In the Gable hybrids, *R. kaempferi*, *R. obtusum* var. *amoenum*, *R. mucronatum* and some of the Kurume and Indicum hybrids were used, and also *R. poukhanense*, which is found wild in Korea and is one of the hardiest of evergreen azaleas, although it can lose most of its leaves in a cold climate. *R. yedoense* is probably a double form of this.

The Glenn Dale hybrids have involved massive crossing, including all the evergreen species and groups of hybrids already mentioned. They were designed to produce flowers as spectacular as those of the tender Indicum hybrids, but on hardy plants to flower from mid-April to mid-June. Hybridizing began in the 1930s and plants became commercially available in the USA after World War II. The flowers may be up to 4½in across, and are mostly single, some frilly-edged, although there are a few hose-in-hose, double and semi-double. Some varieties have striped flowers, presumably deriving from the 'blood' of *R. simsii* var. *vittata*, which was introduced by Robert Fortune in 1850 and has red stripes on a white background. Others have contrasting borders, such as Martha Hitchcock, white edged with magenta, which is one of the relatively few varieties so far commercially available in the UK. There are hundreds on the market in the United States.

'Merlin' is a Glenn Dale azalea, with large magenta flowers borne on a compact plant.

R. indicum was known in Holland in the late seventeenth century; it was probably brought to Europe by ships of the Dutch East India Company. Several colour forms of this are available—red, rose and scarlet at least. Var. *balsaminiflorum* has double flowers. This is *not* the species known to florists as *Azalea indica*—that is *R. simsii*, which comes from China. *R. indicum*, in spite of its name, is a Japanese species; it is known in Japan as the Satsuki azalea—Satsuki being the fifth month, when it blooms, equivalent to our June.

The Satsuki hybrids are different again, and are believed to come from crosses between *R. indicum* and *R. simsii*. They are low growing and late flowering, the flowers are usually single and large, pink or white, and may be self-coloured or striped. They are beautiful but not very hardy and not many are available in Britain, but if they can be obtained and grown successfully, they are very worthwhile because of their late flowering.

Gumpo azaleas are selections of *R. simsii* var. *eriocarpum*. *R. simsii* itself is a greenhouse plant in the British Isles, but this variety is hardier. There are a number of colours available, all with large, frilly flowers, but again they are only suitable for warm areas.

Yet another group of beautiful, but slightly tender, late-flowering (until the end of June) azaleas, consists of the various colour forms of *R. indicum*, such as Hakatoshira (white) and Kokinshita (orange). The azaleas which appear in florist's shops around Christmas are mostly hybrids of *R. indicum* with possibly *R. simsii*, and are sometimes known as Belgian Indian hybrids, as they were bred in Belgium in the nineteenth century. They are not hardy, but can be stood outside in summer. To keep them going from year to year, they must be kept relatively cool in the house (difficult with central heating) and well watered, as they dislike a dry atmosphere. Similar plants have been grown in gardens in the southern states of America for over 100 years.

There are plants called azaleodendrons, where an azalea has been crossed with a rhododendron from another series. Many of these are very old hybrids, and some are very attractive plants. Hybridum is a cross between *R. maximum*, an American species of the Ponticum series, and the American azalea *R. viscosum*, and was bred in 1817. Broughtonii Aureum, Smithii Aureum and Glory of Littleworth are others.

There are 74 species listed in the Azalea series in the RHS Handbook. Most of these, in the wild, are concentrated in two areas, eastern North America and east Asia—mainly China, Japan and Formosa. There are a few isolated species such as *R. luteum*, which is found in the Caucasus and Black Sea area, and *R. occidentale* from the Pacific states of North America. Azalea species are not often seen in gardens except for *R. luteum*, which seems strange as many are very beautiful and some flower very late, into July and even August. The species are described in their series in the next chapter.

If species and hybrid azaleas are to be grown in the same garden it is possibly better to keep them apart as the hybrids are more flamboyant and tend to overwhelm the more subtle beauty of the species. It is generally considered that azaleas are slightly easier to grow than most rhododendrons of other series. They seem to be rather more tolerant of slightly unsuitable conditions. They will not grow in an alkaline soil but, on the whole, do better in soils approaching neutrality. The evergreen types are excellent tub and trough plants and so can be enjoyed on any soil. Azaleas are certainly more tolerant of exposure and the hybrids, at any rate, of drier conditions than would suit the majority of rhododendrons. *R. schlippenbachii*, however, tends not to set flowerbuds after a dry summer and this could well be true of some other species. *R. viscosum* is known in its native haunts as Swamp Honeysuckle, which indicates that it likes a moist soil, and *R. canadense*, *R. vaseyi*, *R. occidentale* and *R. prunifolium* all seem to prefer damp situations.

There must be hundreds of hybrid azaleas available; lists of some of these are given after the descriptions of hybrid rhododendrons.

CHAPTER 8

The Species in their Series

It seems more convenient to deal with the species in their series rather than alphabetically, as this avoids, in many cases, much repetition. Obviously, I cannot attempt to mention all the species in cultivation. The times of flowering given can only be approximate, because of the variation in the weather from season to season, and because the further north one goes, the later plants tend to be. In the same way, the height to which a species can be expected to grow is not always constant. While some, such as the members of the Saluense and Uniflorum series, are always dwarf, others that are normally small can be drawn up if grown under trees, and conversely, tall plants can be dwarfed in an exposed site. I have not divided the series into their subseries, except in the case of the azaleas, where the divisions seem to be of more horticultural importance, but a full list of all the series and subseries and their component species is given at the end of the book. After the name of the series, e stands for elepidote and l for lepidote.

Albiflorum Series (e)
This contains only one species, which is not in general cultivation in the British Isles. It is native to the western states

of North America and has small, hanging white flowers developing from axillary buds.

Anthopogon Series (l)
These are charming plants for small gardens, dwarf and compact with small, dark, aromatic leaves. Except in very hot gardens, they seem to do best in full exposure, and even if the garden is a hot one, they should only have light, dappled shade and not be overhung. The flowers are daphne-like, small and in terminal clusters.

R. anthopogon (H4) is pink and flowers in April; it can grow to about 2ft.

R. cephalanthum (H4) is taller (to about 4ft) and has white flowers, slightly later, in May. Var. *crebreflorum* is dwarfer and the flowers are pink.

R. hypenanthum (H3–4) is a twiggy plant about 2ft tall, very like a yellow *R. anthopogon*.

R. kongboense (H4) is quite rare in cultivation, but at least one specialist nursery is currently offering it. The flowers are a really vivid pink, in April and May.

R. primuliflorum (H4) is tall for this group; it can reach 6ft. The flowers open in April and May, and are yellow or white, occasionally pink.

R. sargentianum (H4) is very compact and grows slowly to about 1ft. It has yellow or creamy-white flowers at the end of April and in May.

R. trichostomum (H3–4) is one of the most beautiful, but is not for colder gardens. It has longer leaves than most—up to 1in—and pink or white flowers in May and June. It grows to about 4ft.

Arboreum Series (e)
All the species in this series are sizeable, ranging from large bushes to fair sized trees.

R. sargentianum s. Anthopogon

R. arboreum (H2–4) is one of the most widely distributed of all rhododendrons in the wild, found throughout the Himalayas into Yunnan and as far south as Ceylon. As might be expected from this, it has several geographical forms, which differ considerably in hardiness. The colour varies from white to pink to red, and unfortunately the red forms seem to be the most tender. It is a magnificent species, if not one for the average garden. It grows over 40ft tall and has leaves up to 8in long, lanceolate, deep glossy green above, with a white or fawn indumentum below. As this was one of the first Himalayan rhododendrons introduced, there are many splendid old trees to be seen in large gardens around the country. Many of the descendants of these trees are not pure *arboreum*, but natural hybrids with other species, but they show their *arboreum* ancestry very plainly. Even when the tree itself is perfectly hardy, it flowers between January and April and, in consequence, there is always the risk of the flowers being frosted. The flowers are bell-shaped and in tight, round trusses of up to 20. Some old specimens have several trunks and give the effect of a thicket rather than a single tree.

R. insigne (H4) forms a bush rather than a tree, it grows slowly up to about 12ft. The leaves are very distinctive, about 5in

R. arboreum s. & ss. Arboreum

104

long, stiff and dark and with a thin, hard, metallic-looking indumentum with a coppery sheen on the underside. The trusses are large, with bell-shaped pink flowers spotted inside and sometimes striped outside, open in May and June.

R. lanigerum (H4) is a shrub or small tree growing to about 20ft, with oblong-lanceolate leaves about 9in long with a white or brown indumentum below. The flowers are in large, round trusses, bell-shaped and purplish, in March and April.

R. zeylanicum (H2–3) is definitely tender, but is a beautiful plant in warm gardens. Seedlings are growing rapidly in our Surrey garden. It forms a tree from 10 to 30ft high, with distinctive spirally marked bark and dark green, bullate leaves with a thick brown indumentum below. The bell-shaped flowers are in dense trusses, usually blood red although there is a pink form. They appear in April and May. I think this is one of the most handsome of all species.

Auriculatum Series (e)

R. auriculatum (H4) is the only species in the series and, beautiful though it is, it is not a plant for the small garden as it forms a spreading tree up to 20ft or more. If it can be grown, it is useful in flowering in July and August; but while it is hardy enough, this is a disadvantage in the north as it does not make new growth until after flowering, and in districts where winter sets in early, this may not ripen sufficiently to set flower-buds for the following year. The name refers to the distinctive shape of the leaves, lobed at the base. The new growth has attractive scarlet bracts. The flowers may be up to 4in across, heavily scented, white or pink. In the USA, it is hardy up to north of Philadelphia.

Azalea Series (e)

This is a large series, divided into 6 subseries, of which 4 are important horticulturally.

R. albrechtii s. Azalea, ss. Canadense

Subseries Canadense. All are deciduous.

R. albrechtii (H4) is a very useful garden species. It has lovely, deep pink, wide open, butterfly-like flowers about 2in across, that open in April, just before the leaves start to unfold. The leaves are in groups of 5 at the ends of the branches, and are bronze when they first open, and colour again slightly, although not spectacularly, in autumn. It can reach 10ft, but is open-growing and not bulky in appearance.

R. canadense (H4) used to be known as *Rhodora canadense* and certainly the flower looks different from that of other rhododendrons, as the lower lip is split almost to the base, giving a two-lipped effect. It grows to about 5ft and has rose purple flowers in April, before the leaves open.

R. pentaphyllum (H4) grows to about 10ft and has leaves in whorls of 5 at the ends of the twigs, which colour well in autumn. It has large rose-pink flowers that open before the leaves.

R. vaseyi (H4) is another tall-growing species, again flowering before the leaves, with paler pink flowers.

Subseries Luteum. Another deciduous group, mostly found in North America, but including the familiar *R. luteum* from around the Black Sea.

R. arborescens (H4) comes from eastern North America, and like several other azaleas, is useful in providing flower later than most of the genus. It has white, long-tubed, scented flowers that are up to 2in across, in groups of 3–6, in June and July. It will grow to 15ft tall.

R. atlanticum (H4) is another American species, but grows only to about 3ft. It is unusual in spreading by stolons. It bears clusters of white or pink, fragrant flowers in May.

R. calendulaceum (H4) from east North America grows to about 15ft and gives splendid autumn colour as well as a fine display of flower in May and June. The flowers have a wide colour range, from yellow through orange and pink to red. This species is one of the ancestors of the Ghent azaleas, and is very hardy.

R. luteum (H4), from the Caucasus and eastern Europe, is one of the commonest and most easily grown of all azaleas, and is a fine garden plant, although it may grow too large for a small garden. It forms an open shrub as much as 12ft tall. The flowers are funnel-shaped, sticky and yellow, with a heavy, honeysuckle perfume, and appear in May, just before the leaves. The leaves colour well in autumn. In the past, this plant has been known as *Azalea pontica* and *Rhododendron flavum*.

R. molle (H4) is best known as one of the parents of the Mollis hybrids. It grows about 4ft tall and has good trusses of yellow or orange flowers, about 2½in in diameter, opening in May.

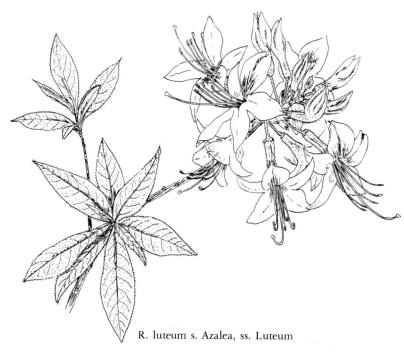

R. luteum s. Azalea, ss. Luteum

R. occidentale (H4), from north-west America, is a large and vigorous grower, flowering in June, with a sweet, strong scent. The flowers are funnel-shaped, pink with a yellow eye, and the leaves colour well in autumn. It is the main parent of the Occidentale hybrids, developed by Koster towards the end of the nineteenth century.

R. speciosum, from east North America, grows to about 6ft and has large clusters of funnel-shaped flowers, orange, apricot or scarlet, in May.

R. viscosum, from the same area, is known as Swamp Honeysuckle. It is a spreading shrub, growing to about 15ft. The long-tubed flowers are white or pink, in clusters of up to a dozen, with a strong, sweet scent. It flowers in June and July.

Subseries Obtusum. 40 species are listed in the current RHS Handbook, but only 17 are in cultivation. Most are evergreen. They have been grown, selected and hybridized for a long time in Japan.

R. kaempferi (H4) is best known as a parent of the Kaempferi hybrids. It is a very variable species, that may be deciduous or semi-evergreen, and can grow as much as 10ft tall. The

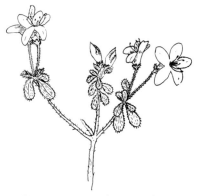

R. kiusianum s. Azalea, ss. Obtusum

flowers can be of almost any colour—red, orange, pink or white—and single, semi-double, or hose-in-hose.

R. kiusianum (H3–4) is believed to be the species from which the Kurume azaleas have been developed. Some plants are quite evergreen; others lose most of their leaves, which turn reddish in autumn. It eventually forms a dense shrub up to about 3ft. The branches are very brittle, and hideously easy to break accidentally while weeding. The leaves are small and hairy, the flowers are also smallish, but freely produced; usually magenta, but occasionally salmon, pink, crimson or white. It is most effective when grown in a group. It flowers in May.

R. obtusum (H4) also has small flowers, profusely borne. There are a number of forms, such as var. *album* with white flowers and var. *amoenum* with magenta flowers, usually hose-in-hose. *Amoenum coccineum* is a form supposed to be more red than magenta. *R. obtusum* is very hardy and flowers in May.

R. serpyllifolium (H4) is of note as having probably the smallest leaves of any rhododendron, only $\frac{1}{4}-\frac{1}{3}$in long—it is only challenged by *R. thymifolium* of the Lapponicum series. Both names mean 'with leaves like thyme'. The flowers are pink, also very small, but it can be attractive in full bloom.

Subseries Schlippenbachii. All the species in this subseries come from Asia, are deciduous and have large flowers.

R. amagianum (H4) grows to about 12ft and has leaves in groups of 3 at the ends of the branches. The flowers are in groups of 3 or 4, orange-red and funnel-shaped, opening in June and July. *R. reticulatum* (H4) is even taller, reaching about 15ft. The leaves are almost as broad as they are long, with the network of veins that gives the species its name standing out clearly on the lower side. The leaves turn purplish in autumn. The flowers appear in April and May before the leaves, and are bright pinkish-purple.

R. schlippenbachii (H4) is an extremely beautiful plant which can make an open bush as much as 15ft tall, although it is often less. The large, saucer-shaped flowers are a clear, pure pink, without any trace of blue or orange, and appear just as the leaves start to unfold in April and May. The leaves colour well in autumn.

Barbatum Series (e)

As the name suggests, the plants of this series have stiff, bristly hairs usually on the twigs and leaf-stalks. Most are attractive plants, some forming graceful small trees. Unfortunately, many are very early-flowering, and so are always liable to be frosted. *R. barbatum* (H3–4) is reputed to form a 60ft tree in the wild, but only reaches 30ft or so in cultivation. It has lovely smooth, reddish bark, and like all the smooth-barked species,

R. schlippenbachii s. Azalea, ss. Schlippenbachii

does not take kindly to any sort of pruning or shaping. The leaf-stalks and branchlets are covered with bristles. The flowers are blood red, in compact trusses, in March.

R. glischrum (H4) also forms a small, spreading tree. The stems and the undersides of the leaves are very bristly. The flowers are pink with a purple blotch in the throat, and are well set off by red calyces and pedicels. They open in April. This too is a very attractive species that could be more widely grown.

R. habrotrichum (H4) is similar, but the undersides of the leaves are hairy only along the midribs. This species seems particularly prone to having its flower-buds frosted, sometimes even in the autumn. The flowers are white or pink, in April. The new growth has attractive red bracts. It forms a large bush, of about 10ft.

R. longesquamatum (H4) has a characteristic furry brown covering on its new growth. The flowers are pink and bell-shaped,

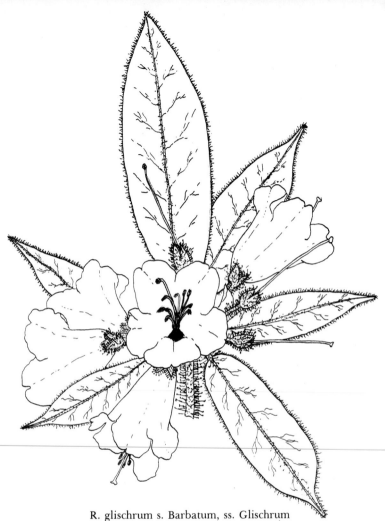

R. glischrum s. Barbatum, ss. Glischrum

in May. It grows to from 3 to more than 10ft tall and is hardy anywhere in Britain, and even in the north-east United States. *R. maculiferum* (H4) forms a shrub or tree up to 20ft. The leaves are light green, paler below, with straggling hairs on the petioles. The flowers are white or pale pink, heavily blotched with purple at the base, in April. *R. morii* (H4) is a lovely plant, with white, red-spotted flowers opening from pink buds. There is a big one at Wisley—it can reach 25ft. It flowers in April.

R. pseudochrysanthum (H4) is slow-growing and compact, with sickle-shaped leaves strongly recurved at the edges, dark green above and white below. The young leaves have a woolly indumentum. The bell-shaped flowers are pink in bud, opening to blush white, spotted with red, in April. It is a plant that takes the eye, in or out of flower.

R. strigillosum (H3-4) forms a large bush rather than a tree and

R. megeratum s. Boothii, ss. Megeratum

although it is March flowering, the unopened buds seem to be frost-hardy and even the open flowers can stand a few degrees. The flowers are a splendid blood red.

Boothii Series (l)

Many of this series are too tender to be of much use in most places, but it does contain one or two valuable plants.

R. leucaspis (H3-4) is a pretty little plant, only reaching about 2ft, with furry leaves and relatively large white flowers with brown anthers. It flowers in February and March and so, of

R. tephropeplum is a plant of great charm, with pink, tubular flowers and dark, willowy leaves, white underneath.

course, is always likely to be frosted in the British Isles, but a plant as small as this can easily be covered if a frosty night seems probable. Although I have not tried it myself, I have seen it suggested that this species and *R. moupinense*, another small, early-flowerer, can be planted in pots which are plunged outside until the buds start to swell (they are not vulnerable until this happens) when they can be taken indoors.

R. megeratum (H3) has flat-faced flowers, like *R. leucaspis*, but they are pale yellow with orange blotches in the throat, and a large, pinkish calyx. The leaves are almost white underneath. It flowers in April and is a plant for warmer parts of the country.

R. tephropeplum (H3–4) is a charming plant growing 3–6ft tall, with dark, willow-shaped leaves, white below, with the scales appearing as black dots. It was first found by Farrer in north-east Burma in 1920, and was later introduced by Forrest and Kingdon-Ward. It used to be known as *R. deliense*. The flowers are tubular-campanulate, usually pink of some shade, but may be magenta, purple or white. It is free-flowering, in April.

R. tephropeplum s. Boothii, ss. Tephropeplum

Campanulatum Series (e)

This Himalayan series resembles the Arboreum series in many ways, but the leaves are usually rounded at the ends instead of pointed.

R. campanulatum (H4) is a very variable species that sometimes forms a large shrub, and sometimes an elegant narrow tree up to about 20ft or more tall. The leaves are dark and glossy with a brown indumentum underneath. The flowers may be white, mauve or purple. It is important to get a good form, such as 'Knaphill'. Var. *aeruginosum*, which used to be considered a separate species, is one of the best of all foliage

R. *campanulatum* is a tree species that does not have very large leaves. It is variable; the flowers may be white, pink, mauve or purple, but are usually spotted. The leaves have a brown indumentum underneath.

plants. The new growth is a metallic, silvery green that later turns to a colour more blue than green.

R. *lanatum* (H4) is a shrub growing to about 6ft with smallish leaves with a thick, woolly, rust-coloured indumentum below. The new growth is very striking, being thickly covered with white or fawn wool. The bell-shaped flowers appear in April and May and are pale yellow, spotted with purple.

Campylogynum Series (l)
At present contains only one species, as several kinds which had specific rank in the past are now merged. It is quite possible that some of these may in time be reinstated; Captain Collingwood Ingram, in the *1969 Rhododendron and Camellia Yearbook* considers that there should be at least 4 species.

R. campanulatum s. Campanulatum

117

R. lanatum s. Campanulatum

R. campylogynum (H3–4) is a very appealing little plant, guaranteed to cause surprise to the uninitiated when they are told it is a rhododendron. All forms have flowers like little thimbles nodding on the ends of erect stalks, but there is considerable variation in the habits of the different forms. The type is a dwarf shrub growing to about 2ft, with leaves about 1in long, and flowers about ¾in, varying in colour from salmon to rose and purple. Var. *myrtilloides* has smaller flowers and grows only about 6in tall. My plant has flowers of a dusky pink, and is smothered with them in May. It has yellow-tipped leaves in autumn and winter, which do not seem to indicate that there is anything wrong as it grows and flowers well. It loses some leaves every winter. Var. *cremastum* is more erect and has leaves that are pale green on both surfaces. Var. *charopeum* has flowers up to 1in long. This species, in one form or other, should be tried in every garden.

Camtscaticum Series (e)

R. camtschaticum (H4) is the only species in this series in cultivation. It is reputedly difficult, but it seems to do well enough

R. campylogynum var. *myrtilloides* is at the other end of the size scale. This plant is growing in a raised bed with *Dryas octopetala* behind it, *Aethionema coridifolia* in front. *R. forrestii* var. *repens* is just appearing at the side.

R. campylogynum var. cremastum s. Campylogynum

in Surrey in an open situation. It is deciduous, and never reaches much more than 6in high with leaves about 2in long, fringed with hairs. It creeps along the ground and has relatively large, reddish-purple flowers with the lower side of the tube deeply cleft. As far as I know, it is the only rhododendron that flowers on the *current* season's growth, rather than on the previous year's. It flowers in May.

R. camtschaticum s. Camtschaticum

Carolinianum Series (l)
This series contains 3 rather similar species native to the eastern USA.
R. carolinianum (H4) is the one most often grown in Britain. It is very hardy but needs good drainage. It has elliptic leaves, very scaley underneath, and pink, long-tubed flowers in clusters of up to 10. There is a white form. It can grow to 6ft and flowers in May and June.

R. minus (H4) and *R. chapmanii* (H4), which are both grown in the States, are very similar to *R. carolinianum* in appearance, but the latter is less hardy as it comes from Florida, where it grows on sandy pine barrens (although it still has an H4 rating for the British Isles), and seems to be able to tolerate much more heat than most rhododendrons.

R. minus s. Carolinianum

Cinnabarinum Series (l)

If I were asked to choose my favourite series of rhododen-dron, this would certainly be on the short list. *R. cinnabarinum* (H4) has flowers often described as being like a *Lapageria*, and for those who know what a *Lapageria* looks like, that is very apt. For those who do not, they are pendant and tubular, waxy-textured, 2 or 3in long, hanging in groups at the end of the branches. It can grow up to about 15ft, but is open and graceful. The foliage is neat and glaucous, with a lovely blue-green effect on the new growth. There are a number of varieties with differently coloured flowers; all are beautiful. The type is cinnabar red; var. *blandfordiiflorum* has yellow

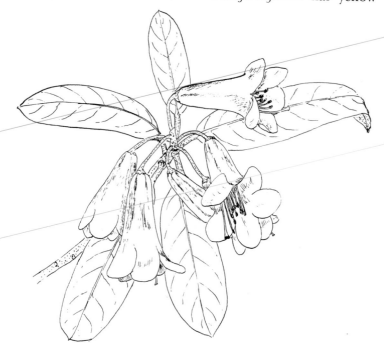

R. cinnebarinum var. blandfordiiflorum
s. Cinnabarinum

flowers flushed with orange-red outside; var. *roylei* has plum-red flowers, slightly shorter, and its close 'Magnificum' has slightly larger flowers. It likes some wind shelter but is perfectly hardy; any form I have seen is worth a place in any garden. It flowers from April–June, depending on the form.

R. concatens (H4) is another lovely species closely allied to the last, in fact there have been suggestions that it is merely a form of it. It is smaller growing, to about 8ft, and has apricot-yellow tubular-campanulate flowers, usually more open than those of *R. cinnabarinum*. It is also a good foliage plant with glaucous leaves and very blue new growth. It flowers in April and May.

R. keysii (H3–4) is slightly tender. The flowers are tubular, not flaring out at all at the ends, red tipped with yellow or orange tipped with red. It grows to about 12ft, and is rather straggly.

R. xanthocodon (H4) again may be just a variety of *R. cinnabarinum* as it is very like a yellow form of the latter, but at present it is considered to be a separate species. It is an open shrub or small tree up to 15ft tall, and flowers in May.

Dauricum Series (l)
R. dauricum (H4) is a twiggy shrub that can grow to 8ft. It is best known as a parent, with *R. ciliatum*, of the hybrid Praecox. The best form is evergreen, but there is also a semi-deciduous form. It flowers from January to March and so should not be planted in a frost pocket, but it is absolutely hardy—it comes from Siberia. The flowers are azalea-like, bright purple-pink. The Russians have split off some varieties of this as separate species, for example *R. sichotense* and some others, but they are not recognized as such in Britain.

R. mucronulatum (H4) is deciduous, with butterfly-like, rosy-purple flowers appearing on the bare branches in January and February. The flowers tend to open in succession, so that

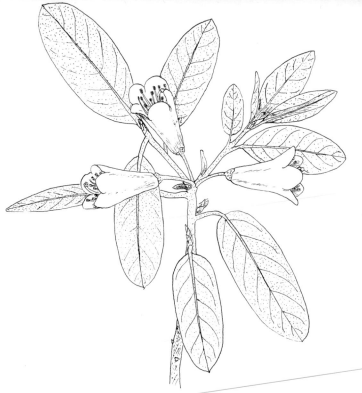

R. xanthocodon s. Cinnebarinum

even if some are frosted, there should still be some show. It too is found in Siberia and Japan, and so is hardy anywhere in Britain and the United States. It makes an open, twiggy shrub up to about 8ft and is best in full exposure.

Edgeworthii Series (l)

This is a small series, with only 2 species of horticultural importance. It is peculiar in that the members have both scales and woolly hairs on the undersides of the leaves.

R. bullatum (H2–4) is a lovely species, with some forms at least hardier than it is often given credit for. The flowers are 4in across, white sometimes tinged with pink, and heavily perfumed. The leaves are very distinctive, with deeply impressed veins giving a puckered effect (this is called bullate) and a thick, brown felty indumentum below. Even its greatest

R. bullatum s. Edgeworthii

admirers could not say it is a tidy grower, as it straggles to a height of about 8ft, but this is a small fault compared to its virtues. It can be grown outside in mild areas, and in cold districts is a lovely plant for a cool greenhouse.

R. edgeworthii (H2–4) is so similar to the last that they are probably one and the same species, the only differences between them being technical ones such as the presence of scales on the calyx of *R. bullatum* but not on that of *R. edgeworthii*. The former comes from Yunnan and Upper Burma, while the latter is found in Sikkim and Bhutan. Both flower in April and May.

Falconeri Series (e)

This is one of the series of 'giants'. All the species have splendid, large, dark green, leathery leaves, with an indumentum beneath. Some can only be grown in the south and west, but others do reasonably well in eastern and northern areas if they are given wind shelter, although the leaves will be smaller. *R. arizelum* (H3–4) makes a small tree up to about 20ft, with elegant tiers of dark, glossy leaves with a brown indumentum below. Like all such species, it is at its best when large enough to enable one to walk under it and look up at the leaves. The foliage effect of such a species is so splendid that one tends to forget that it has flowers as well. These are white or yellow, with a deep crimson blotch at the base, in large trusses, opening in April.

R. basilicum (H3–4) is very similar, but has winged leaf-stalks, and although given the same rating, seems to be not quite so hardy.

R. falconeri (H3–4) is a plant I would attempt to grow in almost any garden. It can be a spreading, many-trunked tree up to 50ft, but often it does not reach even half that size. The trunk has reddish-brown bark, the leaves are 1ft long or more, with a rich brown indumentum below. The young shoots are

R. fictolacteum is a splendid tree species, with large, leathery leaves, brown underneath, and purple-throated creamy flowers.

covered with a pale brown fur which soon rubs off the upper surfaces. It produces large, round trusses of creamy-yellow, bell-shaped flowers in April and May. This is one of the hardiest of the large-leaved species, but should always be given as much shelter as possible. The new growth appears in June, and in the south of England, this can be a problem if it coincides with a hot spell, as the new leaves may be mis-shapen. This is less likely to happen if it is well sheltered, and a smallish plant can be watered and sprayed.

R. fictolacteum (H4) again can make a tree of 40ft. It is slightly hardier than the last species, but the leaves are usually not so large. It is a much more variable species, some forms are rather mediocre, while others are most impressive. The flowers are again bell-shaped, in large trusses, white, cream or pink with a purple blotch, opening in April and May.

R. hodgsonii (H4) grows as a small tree to 20ft. The new

R. fictolacteum s. Falconeri

growth is covered with a silvery film which remains in patches on the upper surfaces of the mature leaves, making a good distinguishing point. The flowers are pink to magenta, occasionally white, opening in April.

R. rex (H4) is a fine tree species, growing to over 40ft. It was originally classified as a large-leaved form of R. fictolacteum, but now has specific rank. The flowers, which open in April and May, are white or pink with a crimson blotch. It is reputed to be able to stand more cold than most of the large-leaved species.

Ferrugineum Series (H4)
This contains 3 species, all native to Europe, *R. ferrugineum* (H4) is found in the Alps and the Pyrenees, and is well-known as the alpenrose. It grows to about 4ft and has leaves $1-1\frac{1}{2}$in long, covered with dense, rusty scales underneath. The rose to crimson flowers are in small clusters, borne in June. It is hardy anywhere in Britain, but in America, seems to find the east coast climate too hot and dry.

R. hirsutum (H4) has the distinction of being the first rhododendron known to have been cultivated. It is very similar to the last species, and is also called alpenrose. The main difference is that the leaves are fringed with hairs, and in the wild it grows on limestone. Because of this, it might be worth attempting to grow it in a garden where one would not try other rhododendrons. *R. kotschyi* (H3–4) comes from the

R. ferrugineum s. Ferrugineum

Transylvanian Alps, and is not often seen in gardens. It is very like the last 2 species.

Fortunei Series (e)

This series has been used extensively in hybridization, and many of the species are fine plants in their own right. The leaves are usually smooth and rounded at both ends, not unlike those of the Thomsonii series. The flowers have often 7 or 8 lobes, instead of the usual 5, with twice the number of stamens.

R. calophytum (H4) forms a 30ft tree with distinctive and elegant long, narrow leaves. The flowers are in large trusses, white or pink with a red blotch, and open in March and April.

R. decorum (H3–4) grows to about 20ft, either as a tree or large shrub. The scented pink or white flowers are in large trusses and may be as much as 5in across, but the forms with the largest flowers tend to be the most tender. The hardier forms can be grown in most parts of Britain. Cox's Uranium Green is a clone with chartreuse-coloured flowers. The various forms flower from April to June.

R. diaprepes (H3) is another tree species with white, scented flowers that can be 6in in diameter. It is hardy only in the south and west of the British Isles, but where it can be grown, it is useful for its late flowering time, June and July.

R. discolor (H3–4) also flowers in June and July, but is more a large shrub than a tree. It flowers very freely when mature, and is hardier than the last species. The funnel-shaped flowers are white or blush pink, about 4in in diameter, and fragrant. It has been used a lot as a parent.

R. fargesii and *R. oreodoxa* (both H4) are so similar that they can be treated together; the latter usually has narrower leaves. Both are shrubs reaching 15–20ft, with pink or lilac flowers borne so profusely that it is best to dead-head as much of the plant as can be reached. They are perfectly

R. fargesii stands in a pool of its own fallen, lilac blossom. This specimen has been given plenty of room and has an elegant, symmetrical shape.

hardy, but because they flower in March and April, should be given as frost-free a site as possible. They are hardy in the USA as far north as New York.

R. fortunei (H4) was the first Chinese rhododendron to be introduced to Britain, by Robert Fortune in 1856. One of the original plants from this introduction is still growing in Windsor Great Park. It forms a tree of up to 30ft, with loose trusses of opulent, 4in, funnel-shaped, rather frilly-edged, pale pink scented flowers. It flowers in May and is hardy anywhere in the British Isles and the west coast of the United States, and on the east coast as far north as Boston.

R. griffithianum (H1–3) is not a plant that many people will be able to grow, but must be mentioned. It makes a tree of up to 20ft, and has amongst the largest flowers in the genus, sumptuous wide open bells, pink or white, often

R. fargesii s. Fortunei, ss. Oreodoxa

fragrant. Unfortunately it is hardy only in the south and west of Britain, and even there, needs a sheltered position. It is a parent of some famous hybrids, such as Penjerrick and the Loderi grex. It is May-flowering.

R. orbiculare (H4) is one of the most distinctive of all rhododendrons, and an excellent garden plant. The leaves are almost round and are a bright, fresh green. The 7-lobed, bell shaped flowers are rose pink, opening in April. It forms a dense, spreading bush, reputedly up to 10ft tall, but in most

R. vernicosum s. & ss. Fortunei

gardens it does not approach that height. It is hardy anywhere in Britain—the American rating is to −5°F.

R. praevernum (H4) is a shrub or small tree up to 12ft, flowering in February to April. It has a bell-shaped white flowers,
sometimes flushed pink, with a red blotch.

R. serotinum (H4) is not often seen, but is worth a mention
as the latest flowering species in the genus, blooming at the
end of August into September, and sometimes on until
November. It grows to about 15ft and has striking bronze
new growth, and white flowers marked with red inside.

R. sutchuense (H4) makes a shrub or tree up to 20ft, with leaves 1ft long, dark above and pale below. It has large trusses of bell-shaped pink or lilac flowers, spotted with purple, in February and March.

R. vernicosum (H4) is a variable species, with frilly white or pink flowers, sometimes spotted with red, and very waxy leaves. It flowers in April and May.

Fulvum Series (e)
This contains only 2 species.

R. fulvum (H4) is a superb foliage plant that forms a small tree of about 20ft. The young shoots are covered with a brownish fur. The mature leaves are about 10in long, dark and glossy above with a bright, orange-brown indumentum below. It is a lovely sight when blown by a breeze, making a rippling pattern of green and brown. Some forms have good flowers as well, with large, round trusses of pink flowers, sometimes blotched or spotted with purple. It flowers in March and April.

R. uvariifolium (H4) has a less striking indumentum, but has a beautiful, silvery young growth. The flowers appear in March and April and are white or pink, in large, tight trusses.

Glaucophyllum Series (l)
This is a series of semi-dwarfs, reaching 5ft at most, with dark, very aromatic foliage.

R. brachyanthum (H4) grows very slowly to about 3ft—I have a plant which has achieved 3in in 6 years. The flowers, which open in June and July, are small, bell shaped and greenish yellow, but very freely borne.

R. charitopes (H4) is a compact shrub up to 3 or 4ft. The flowers are in clusters of up to 6, pink flecked with red. Its main flowering season is April and May, but it often produces a second crop in the autumn.

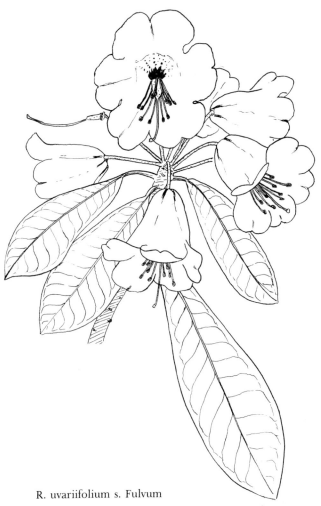

R. uvariifolium s. Fulvum

R. glaucophyllum (H3–4) is an attractive species that can reach 4ft, with grey-green aromatic leaves, glaucous beneath. The bell-shaped flowers are pink, in clusters of up to 10, usually fewer. Var. *luteiflorum* has bright yellow, narrower flowers and darker green leaves.

135

R. glaucophyllum var. luteiflorum s. Glaucophyllum

Grande Series (e)

This is the series with the largest leaves in the genus. As might be expected, while they can be grown in other parts, they need the humid, mild atmosphere of the south and west to be seen at their best.

R. *macabeanum* (H3–4) is the hardiest of the series, but it too needs shelter, preferably woodland, as its leaves are usually about 1 ft long and half as wide, leathery dark green with conspicuous veins above, and a whitish woolly indumentum below. The new shoots are silvery with red bud scales. The flowers have an unusual pouched shape and are borne profusely in large trusses. They are cream to bright yellow in colour, and appear in March and April.

R. *sinogrande* (H3–4) is not a plant for most gardens, but it cannot be left out, as it is one of the most magnificent species in the genus. Its splendour lies in its leaves which, in a young plant, may be as much as 3 ft long and 1 ft across. When the tree reaches flowering size, the leaves tend to be smaller. They are dark and leathery, covered with a silvery indumentum when young, which later disappears from the top surface but remains underneath. It can make a tree 30ft tall, but must have almost complete wind shelter. There are some fine specimens in Britain, particularly in west coast gardens. In a plant like this, flowers seem an irrelevance, but they are produced in April, in trusses about 1ft long, bell shaped, creamy with a red blotch. Var. *boreale* has yellow flowers.

Griersonianum Series (e)
R. griersonianum (H3–4) is the only species in the series. It is reputedly tender, but it grows in Surrey in full exposure without the slightest trouble, and is also grown successfully in eastern Scotland. It is a rather open and straggly grower, up to 8ft with long-tubed, large flowers of a soft yet intense shade of geranium scarlet. The leaves are dark and pointed, with a buff indumentum below. The flower and foliage buds look very much alike, and are very distinctive, long and pointed with many bracts—a feature inherited by many of the hybrids of which *R. griersonianum* is a parent. It has been used more than any other species in hybridization, but although many of the offspring are beautiful, none have quite the beauty of flower of the species itself. In spite of its hardiness classification, I would attempt to grow *R. griersonianum* in any garden I had. I suspect that plenty of sun to ripen the wood and plenty of water in the growing season are important. There is no risk of flower buds being frosted, as it flowers in June.

Heliolepis Series (l)
This series is not very much grown in gardens, but nevertheless contains some good plants.
R. desquamatum (H4) and *R. rubiginosum* (H4) are very similar, differing only slightly in the pattern of the scales on the undersides of the leaves, that are so thick there as to give a brownish colour. Both are very free-flowering, and a plant smothered

R. griersonianum s. Griersonianum

in mauve or lilac flowers in April is a handsome sight. The flowers are in loose trusses, often spotted with red, the leaves are dark, willowy and aromatic. Both grow to 20ft or more. R. fumidum (H4) and R. heliolepis (H4) are again very much like the last two species, but are smaller, and flower later, in May and June.

Irroratum Series (e)

This is one of the largest series, centred in Yunnan. It is not one of the more important series horticulturally, however, as although several of the species are very beautiful, most are tender.

R. rubiginosum s. Heliolepis

R. aberconwayi is a species that is fairly new to cultivation. It is beautiful, hardy and free-flowering.

R. aberconwayi (H4) is a relatively recent introduction; seeds were first sent to England in 1937, and it is absolutely hardy. It grows up to 8ft tall, with an open habit, and has hard and oddly brittle leaves—this is already obvious in seedlings a year old. The flowers are lovely, large and saucer-shaped, pink or white, often with crimson spots. It flowers in May and June, and is reputed to do well in drier areas.

R. elliottii (H2–3) has flowers that must be about the brightest red of any rhododendron's, but it is a cool house plant anywhere except in Cornwall and the west of Wales and Scotland, the southern part of the Pacific Coast of the USA and parts of New Zealand and Australia. It grows 10 or 12ft tall, and flowers in May and June. It has been used quite a lot recently in hybridization, as has the next species, with the hope of linking the superb flower colour to greater hardiness.

R. eriogynum (H2–3) again has brilliant red flowers in June, waxy and tubular-campanulate, in trusses of up to 16. It too is a greenhouse plant in most places.

R. facetum (H2–3) is similar in flower, but makes a tree of up to 30ft.

R. irroratum (H4) can grow as a shrub or tree up to 25ft and has large trusses of flowers which are rather variable in colour—white, yellowish or suffused with pink. It flowers early, in March and April.

R. pogonostylum (H2), in spite of its rating, grows outside at Wisley. It makes a tree of up to 15ft tall, with hard, stiff leaves, and has trusses of pink, tubular-campanulate flowers, pouched at the base, spotted red.

R. venator (H3–4) is the hardiest of the red-flowered species in this series. It has bright scarlet tubular, waxy flowers in loose trusses, that contrast beautifully with the dark, glossy leaves. It flowers in May and June, grows to about 8ft, and is a very handsome plant indeed.

R. pogonostylum s. & ss. Irroratum

R. venator s. Irroratum, ss. Parishii

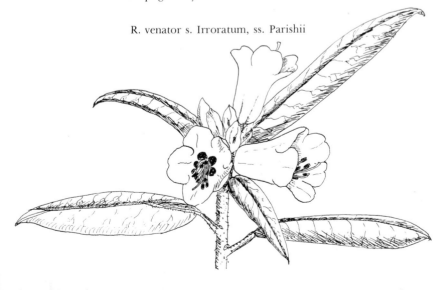

Lacteum Series

R. lacteum is a species that is not recommended except for someone who likes a challenge and does not mind disappointment. In its best forms, it has possibly the brightest yellow flowers of any rhododendron, in great, globular trusses, but it is one of the most temperamental species in the genus, growing slowly, and dying perversely just as it seems to be settling down. It is supposed to do best on a soil that is very acid indeed, as much as pH 3·5. It can grow to 30ft, but is usually less, and has handsome leaves with a brown indumentum. It is one of the few plants where grafting is recommended, as it is reputedly easier to grow on a Ponticum stock. It flowers in April and May.

R. wightii (H3–4) is rather like a watered down version of the last species, but it is rather better tempered.

Lapponicum Series (l)

While this series contains no spectacular species, it is one of the most useful in the genus, and there must be very few gardens where any species rhododendrons are grown that does not contain at least one of them. Many are very similar, and as there are over 50 members of the series, I shall only mention a few of them. Most have flowers of some shade of mauve and small, rather greyish-green, leaves, all but two are dwarf usually under 2ft tall, much branched. They are very much high altitude plants, most coming from the mountains of Yunnan and Szechwan, although *R. lapponicum* is found in Lapland.

R. chryseum (H4) is particularly useful in having yellow flowers, in April and May.

R. drumonium (H4) has bluish-purple or mauve flowers in ones or twos in April, and leaves covered with brown scales on the underside.

R. edgarianum (H4) is the latest of the series to flower, in May and June. Although taller than some, up to 3ft, the leaves are tiny, only about ⅓in long. The flowers are purplish.

R. flavidum (H4) is a paler yellow than *R. chryseum*, and flowers in March.

R. fastigiatum (H4) is usually a rather stiff, upright little shrub up to about 3ft, with mauve to purple flowers. It is hardy, free-flowering and easily obtainable, but the rather straggly growth makes it less desirable than the more compact *R. impeditum*. It flowers in April and May.

R. hippophaeoides (H4) can sometimes reach 5ft. It prefers a

R. drumonium s. Lapponicum

fairly moist site and is best in full exposure (as indeed the whole series is) as shade tends to make it leggy. The leaves are up to 1½in long and the flowers, in March and April, are in various shades of lavender, mauve and pink.

R. idoneum (H4) flowers in April and May and has white-throated, dark blue-purple flowers.

R. impeditum (H4) is one of the best of the series, good-tempered, free-flowering and neat in habit. It grows to about 1ft high in a compact mound. The leaves are small, very scaley on both surfaces, grey-green when young and blue-green when mature. The flowers are mauve to blue-purple—the nearer to blue, the better. It flowers in April and May and is hardy anywhere in Britain. Apparently, while hardy on the east coast of the USA, it dislikes the dry summer heat there, but does well anywhere on the west coast north of California. *R. intricatum* (H4) is another useful, lavender-flowered dwarf; April flowering, and rather like *R. impeditum*.

R. microleucum (H4) is the only white-flowered member of the

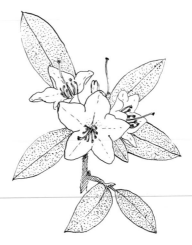

R. ravum s. Lapponicum

series. It is possible that it is not a true species, but an albino form of one of the other members. Plants in cultivation have all originated from one seedling grown at Exbury. However, it remains a useful little plant, growing to 1½ft, with light green leaves and clusters of ¾in white flowers in April.

R. ravum (H4) and the similar *R. cuneatum* (H4) are the two rather anomalous members of the series. They are larger—the latter can grow to 10ft—and have bigger leaves, rather a pleasant grey-green, and pink flowers in April and May.

R. rupicola (H4) has flowers of a strong crimson-purple, and elliptic leaves, broader than those of most of the series, brown underneath. It flowers in April and May.

R. russatum (H4) is one of the best, and is taller than most. The flowers are relatively large, in groups of 4–6, rich purple with a white throat. The leaves are brown and scaly below; it flowers in April and May. Var. *cantabile*, which used to have specific rank, is smaller and more compact and lacks the white throat. *R. scintillans* (H4) is another outstanding species in its best forms. The colour varies from the usual lavender to a really intense, almost royal blue; the FCC form is particularly good. It is free-flowering (April and May) and vigorous, growing eventually to about 3ft.

Lepidotum Series (l)

R. baileyi (H3–4) is a very untidy grower, straggling to 5ft or so, but the flowers, which are flat-faced and open in May, are a really intense purple—an unusual colour in any plant. It seems to be not very hardy, as some seedlings I had all succumbed in their third winter. This was quite a mild one, but such frosts as there were, came early on, in November. They were quite unscathed the previous winter, which had been much more severe, but with most of the frost in January and February.

R. lepidotum (H3–4) is widely distributed in the wild, in Nepal, Burma, Szechwan and Yunnan, and like most such species, is very variable. It can grow to 5ft, but is often a dwarf. All I have seen have purple flowers, but they can be pink, crimson, yellow or white. It flowers in June.

R. lowndesii (H3–4) was only discovered in 1950, in Nepal. It grows only about 1ft tall, is deciduous, with hairy leaves, and has wide-open yellow flowers with a few red spots, in June and July.

R. baileyi shows its lepidote scales clearly on its flower-stalks. Some idea of the variety of shape of flowers found in the genus is given when these flat-faced flowers (which are rich purple in colour) are compared to those of 'Grierdal' or *R. cinnabarinum*.

Maddenii Series (l)

This is a large series with some lovely species, but very few are hardy outside in most parts of Britain. They do well in the Melbourne area of Australia, the San Francisco area of the USA and much of New Zealand. They make very good cool greenhouse plants although some are straggly growers.

R. burmanicum (H1–3) grows to 6ft and has greenish-yellow fragrant flowers in April and May.

R. ciliatum (H3–4) must be the most widely grown of the series. It is a delightful plant, usually fairly compact, but can grow to as much as 6ft in a moist climate, particularly if shaded by trees. It has a luxuriant and exotic look about it, with large, frilly, perfumed, pale pink flowers, and glossy dark leaves fringed with hairs. It flowers in March and early

April, but for some reason is very rarely frosted in our garden, even when frost harms species flowering slightly earlier or slightly later. It is hardy in all but the coldest parts of Britain.

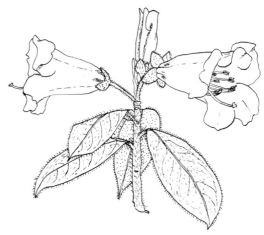

R. ciliatum s. Maddenii, ss. Ciliicalyx

R. ciliicalyx (H1–2) has large, fragrant white or blush pink flowers in March and April, and grows to about 10ft.

R. crassum (H2–4) is very variable in hardiness, with some forms at least as hardy as the more widely grown *R. ciliatum*. The flowers are heavily scented and as much as 4in across, in trusses of 4 or 5, usually white but occasionally pink. It has very attractive glossy leaves. It flowers in June and July, and can reach 15ft.

R. dalhousiae (H1–2) grows to 10ft, and has perfumed creamy-yellow flowers in May and June.

R. fletcherianum (H4) is another of the hardy species. It grows to about 4ft and has hairy leaves and branches and pale yellow flowers in March and April.

147

R. formosum (H2–3) has white flowers with a spicey scent, flushed with yellow and pink and sometimes with 5 red stripes on the outside, in May and June. It can grow to 10ft. I have seen this growing well outside in west of Scotland gardens, but for most places, it is a cool house plant, as the rating suggests.

R. lindleyi (H1–3) has funnel-shaped flowers 4 or 5in across, sometimes with a yellow blotch in the throat, with a strong, spicy scent, in April and May. It grows to about 10ft and again can only be grown outside in the extreme south and west.

R. maddenii (H2–3) grows to 8 or 9ft and has large, fleshy white flowers in clusters of 2 or 4, in June.

R. megacalyx (H2–3) would need a large greenhouse, as it makes a small tree up to 16ft. It has white, pink-tinged, spicy scented flowers in April and May.

R. megacalyx has the opulent, exotic appearance typical of tender rhododendrons. The large calyx that gives the species its name shows up well.

R. nuttallii (H1–2) grows to 15ft or more and has the largest flowers of any species in cultivation, up to 6in across and 5in long. The leaves have deeply impressed veins on top and are purple-bronze when young. It has attractive smooth, red-brown bark, and flowers in April and May. There is a large plant in the cool greenhouse in the Savill Garden in Windsor Great Park.

R. rhabdotum (H1–2) grows to 12ft and has creamy white flowers with red stripes down the outside of the petals, often flushed with yellow within, in May to July.

R. taggianum (H1–2) grows to 8ft, and has funnel-shaped flowers 4in in diameter, white with a yellow basal blotch, heavily perfumed, in April and May.

R. valentinianum (H3–4) is rather like a yellow flowered *R. ciliatum*, and grows to about 3ft. Where it can be grown, it is a useful plant with its dwarf habit and gay flowers that appear in April.

Moupinense Series (l)

This is a series of only 3 species, of which one is in cultivation.

R. moupinense (H4) is one of the loveliest of the early species, but is unfortunately liable to be frosted as it flowers in February and March. However, as it is small—it can reach 4ft, but does so slowly—it can be covered at night. The buds only seem susceptible after they have started to swell, and the plant itself is perfectly hardy. The foliage is good, with neat, dark glossy leaves, bronze in the new growth. The flowers are 2in across, usually white although they can be pink, sometimes with red spots. It has been used a lot in hybridization.

Neriiflorum Series (e)

This is a very important series from the gardening point of view. The flowers are almost always tubular-campanulate in loose trusses, waxy textured, and are often red.

R. aperantum (H4) grows slowly to about 2ft, and has a greater spread. It is rather like a larger edition of the better known *R. forrestii*. The flowers are 2in long, and very variable in colour—white, yellow, pink, orange or crimson. It apparently makes sheets of colour growing wild in Upper Burma, but is very reluctant to flower in cultivation. If it does, it is in April and May.

R. beanianum (H3–4) is again variable in colour, the best forms are red. The foliage is dark and glossy, with deeply impressed veins and a brown indumentum below. It is a rather straggly grower up to 8ft and flowers from March to May.

R. catacosum (H4) is a beautiful species, not often grown. It grows to about 9ft; the young growth is covered with a white or brown wool and the mature leaves have a thick brown indumentum below. It has trusses of up to 9 bright-red, bell-shaped flowers in March and April.

R. chamae-thomsonii (H4) is a useful small rhododendron that grows slowly to about 3ft. It is quite variable; the flowers can be scarlet, pink, orange or even white, but are usually deep crimson, in groups of 1–4. The leaves are dark and glossy, often with a reddish stalk, typically 1–2in long, but there is a small-leaved form known as var. *chamaethauma*. It usually flowers in April.

R. dichroanthum (H4) is an unusual looking plant with hanging, tubular-campanulate flowers, orange through salmon to pink, that are sometimes rather hidden by the leaves. It forms a dense, spreading shrub up to 6ft. It has been used a lot in hybridization, as it imparts this orange colour to its offspring (eg Fabia). The leaves have a white indumentum below. It flowers in May and June.

R. forrestii (H4) is a slow growing, prostrate shrub, with dark glossy leaves, that likes to mould itself over stones as it grows. The flowers are splendid, bell-shaped and scarlet, large for such a small plant, but unfortunately many forms are shy to flower. Any intending purchaser should make sure that his plant is of a free-flowering clone. A plant in full flower cascading down a bank is an unforgettable sight. Var. *repens*, which differs from the type in having leaves pale green below instead of purplish, is the kind most usually available, and is completely prostrate. Var. *tumescens* is rather dome-shaped in the centre, though the outer branches are still creeping. *R. forrestii* should be checked over from time to time and any debris that has collected in the centre of the plant should be removed, as this may make it start to rot. The plants make such a dense mat that dead leaves etc cannot fall through the branches to the ground.

R. haematodes (H4) is a species with few, if any, faults. It flowers in May and June and so does not get frosted, and it is absolutely hardy. It can grow to 10ft, but is more often less than half that height. The leaves are dark above with a woolly, red-brown indumentum below, and the flowers, freely borne once the plant matures, are in trusses of 6–12, waxy and usually brilliant red, although there are white or pink forms.

R. neriiflorum (H3–4) is an excellent garden rhododendron, usually quite hardy in spite of the rating. It is a slow grower, reaching 6ft eventually, though there is a form, var. *euchaites*, that grows to 15ft. The leaves are bright green above and white below. The flowers are in loose trusses of up to a dozen, tubular-campanulate, $1\frac{1}{2}$–2in long, bright red and waxy (this heavy texture means they last well), sometimes with a large red calyx. It flowers in April and May and does best in semi-shade.

R. sanguineum (H4) is an extremely variable species, and many plants which used to be species in their own right, such as *R. didymum*, are now considered to be subspecies of it. The type grows to about 3ft and has clusters of rich red flowers,

R. neriiflorum s. & ss. Neriiflorum

but unfortunately can be reluctant to flower. Var. *didymum* is slow-growing, with smaller leaves, and flowers of so dark a red as to seem almost black—it is best placed where the sun can shine through the flowers. Ten subspecies in all are listed in the handbook.

R. sperabile (H3–4) is a shrub that may be from $1\frac{1}{2}$ to 6ft tall. It is less hardy than *R. neriiflorum*. The leaves have a thick brownish indumentum below, the flowers are red, thick and fleshy, opening in April and May. There is sometimes a second show in the autumn.

Ponticum Series (e)

This series has been rather neglected in Britain, perhaps because the feral *R. ponticum* is so common, but it is much more highly regarded in America, which has some native members, partly because of its hardiness. Some of the species are very handsome, although others are certainly rather pedestrian.

R. adenopodum (H4) although it comes from Szechwan, is not one of the best, although a plant as hardy as this is always useful. It grows densely to about 10ft, and has long, fairly narrow leaves with a grey to fawn felty indumentum below. The flowers are in loose trusses, pink and usually spotted, in April and May.

R. brachycarpum (H4) grows to about 10ft, with bright green leaves, furry white in the new growth, and a fawn or brown indumentum below. There are up to 20 funnel-shaped flowers in a truss, creamy-white to pale pink. It flowers in June and July.

R. catawbiense (H4) is much more highly thought of in the United States, where a number of colour forms have been selected, than in Britain. In its better forms, it can be a pleasant plant and can withstand up to 60° of frost. Oddly enough, Woolworths often seem to stock it. The leaves tend to be rather a yellowish green, but the trusses can be quite large, the colour varying from pinkish-mauve to bluish-mauve. There is a white variety. This species was used extensively in the nineteenth century for hybridization, to pass on its hardiness and late flowering time (June) to the early and tender Asians. Unfortunately, it also tended to pass on its magentaish colour and a propensity to attack by rhododendron bug.

R. caucasicum (H4) is not very often grown, although the old variety, Cunningham's Sulphur, is possibly a form of it. It grows to about 10ft and has yellowish or pale pink flowers, very thin textured, in an elongated truss.

R. chrysanthum (H4) was one of the earliest rhododendrons known, but now is not often seen. It grows little more than

R. degronianum s. Ponticum, ss. Caucasicum

1ft tall and is very hardy—it comes from Siberia. The flowers are in trusses of 5–9, pale yellow and rather flimsy in texture, opening in May and June. It does not like too hot a sun.

R. degronianum (H4) is a spreading shrub up to about 5ft, with narrow leaves with a red-brown indumentum below, and pale pink flowers in April and May. It too is very hardy and comes from Japan.

R. makinoi (H3–4) is a plant I like very much, it is one of the most distinctive in the genus, with narrowly lanceolate leaves, about 7in long and less than 1in across, with recurved margins and a tawny indumentum, that give the plant a strangely exotic look. The new growth is very late, in August and September, and is covered with white or tawny wool. The

154

flowers open in May and June and are clear pink in good trusses. I cannot think why this species is so seldom grown.

R. *maximum* (H4) is rarely grown in the British Isles as there are so many better species available, but it is popular in the United States, where it is a native, because of its extreme hardiness. It grows to about 15ft and the flowers, opening in July, are pink or white. It is reputed to be very shade tolerant.

R. *metternichii* (H4) is very like R. *degronianum*, in fact many plants of the latter are wrongly labelled as the former. The only difference seems to be that R. *metternichii* has 7-lobed flowers, whereas those of R. *degronianum* have 5 lobes. The true R. *metternichii* is rare in cultivation.

R. *ponticum* (H4) must be the best known of all rhododendrons, as it is naturalized in so many places. The better forms have flowers of a good deep mauve, approaching purple and good dark, glossy foliage. It makes a useful windbreak or large hedge.

R. *smirnowii* (H4) is one of the few European rhododendrons, as it comes from around the Caucasus. It is a good foliage plant, with the new growth covered by a silvery-white indumentum, which remains on the underside of the mature leaves. It grows to 8–10ft and again is very hardy. The flowers are rose-pink, rather frilly round the edges.

R. *ungernii* (H4) comes from the same region and is very similar, but has more compact trusses.

R. *yakusimanum* (H4) is a species that is currently very fashionable. A well-grown specimen is certainly beautiful, even if it is so neat that it looks like a woman who has just come out of a hairdresser's. It has globose trusses coloured like appleblossom, and makes a compact shrub, perhaps 4ft high, with rather brittle leaves recurved at the margins, and a pale brown indumentum below. The new growth is covered with white fur. I think it is too slow-growing; mine grows little more than 1in a year, if that, and after 6 years has not yet

R. yakusimanum is a species which always remains compact, and has large trusses of flowers coloured like apple blossom.

flowered. Perhaps it does not like the conditions, but it has behaved the same way in two very different gardens and two sites in my present one. Possibly this is illogical, as I do not mind waiting for the large species to flower; but there one can see their growth year by year. However, some people's must grow more, as I have seen quite large specimens. It has been used a lot in recent years in hybridization, but not many of its offspring are as yet on the market. There are a number, not yet named, growing in the Savill Garden, Windsor Great Park.

Micranthum Series (l)
R. micranthum (H4) is the only species. It is not widely grown, but is hardy and quite pretty in its general effect. The individual flowers are tiny, not much more than $\frac{1}{4}$in across, but

are closely packed and the plant gives an effect rather like a *Spiraea*. It grows to 6ft and flowers in May and June, sometimes into July.

Saluense Series (l)
This is a useful series of real dwarfs. The flowers are almost reddish-purple, very flat, wide open with a short tube, and large for the size of the plants. The leaves are small, scaly below and often fringed with hairs.
R. calostratum (H4) is a desirable plant for any garden. It is one of the tallest in the series, growing to 3 or 4ft, with small, grey-green leaves that set off the rosy-purple flowers very well. It flowers in May and June, and does not like too hot and dry a situation.
R. keleticum (H4) is a pleasant little plant, with shiny green leaves and flowers held well clear of the foliage. Some forms are quite prostrate while others form a low mound. The purple flowers are held well above the foliage, but tend to face downwards. It flowers in May and June.

R. keleticum s. Saluense

R. nitens (H4) has paler flowers than the others in the series. It grows up to 1½ft and flowers in June and July.

R. prostratum (H4) as the name suggests, hugs the surface of the ground. Its leaves and flowers are slightly larger than those of *R. keleticum*, otherwise it is very much like it, and flowers in May.

R. radicans (H4) is always prostrate, with smaller leaves than the other species, and for practical purposes, seems to differ from *R. keleticum* only in having flowers that face upwards, which makes it more effective. It too flowers in May and June.

R. saluense (H4) grows to about 4ft, although there are some dwarfer forms. The habit can be upright or spreading. The flowers are similar to those of the rest of the series, the leaves are larger—1½in long and 1in wide. It is hardy anywhere in Britain and in the north-east United States as far as cold is concerned, but it does not like the hot summers there. It flowers in April and May.

Scabrifolium Series (l)

This is quite a small series, only one of which, *R. racemosum*, is widely grown. The flowers are axillary instead of terminal as in most rhododendrons.

R. hemitrichotum (H4) grows to 4ft and has leaves hairy above, scaly and glaucous below (hence, presumably, the name, which means 'half hairy'). The pale pink flowers open from red buds in April.

R. pubescens (H4) and *R. spiciferum* (H3) are probably one species. They grow from 3–6ft high and have pink, funnel-shaped flowers in April and May, and hairy leaves.

R. racemosum (H4) must be one of the most widely grown of all rhododendron species, and while it is a pleasant enough plant, I would say it was overrated. It is quite a variable plant, some forms grow to 6ft or more, while others remain at 2 or 3ft. The flowers may be white, or pale or deep pink, the paler forms often being darker round the edges of the petals. The individual flowers are smallish, but freely borne. The leaves are greyish-green and some forms have red stems. *Forrest 19404* is a good dwarf form with deeper coloured flowers than most. *R. racemosum* flowers at the end of March and in April.

R. racemosum s. Scabrifolium

R. scabrifolium s. Scabrifolium

R. scabrifolium (H3) is similar, but not so hardy, and taller—up to 10ft.

R. spinuliferum (H2–3) is only hardy in mild parts of the country, but it is so unusual looking a plant that it is worth a mention. The flowers are completely tubular, with protruding stamens, about 1in long, of varying shades of red, and stand upright like candles on a cake. It flowers in April.

Taliense Series (e)

According to Kingdon-Ward, 'The beginner is cautioned after hankering after any of the "Taliense" type.' The reason for this is that they are so slow to flower. This is presumably why they are not widely grown, as many are excellent foliage plants.

R. adenogynum (H4) grows slowly to 9ft or so, it has long narrow leaves with a brown indumentum below. The flowers are in large trusses, opening in April, and are pink marked with red.

R. bureauvii (H4) is a superb foliage plant. It grows to about 8ft, and has dark leathery leaves with a bright, rusty-orange, woolly indumentum underneath. The young growth has a fawn indumentum. The pink or white tubular-campanulate flowers are in compact trusses, and appear in April and May.

R. detonsum (H4) grows to about 12ft and has narrow leaves with a brown indumentum. The flowers are up to $2\frac{1}{2}$in long, in loose trusses, pink spotted crimson, opening in May. This is an attractive plant.

R. gymnocarpum (H4) only reaches about 4ft and is unusual in this series in having red flowers. They are bell-shaped, in loose trusses, opening in April. The leaves are leathery with a brown indumentum.

R. roxieanum (H4) is a very variable species, but is an attractive foliage plant. The leaves are linear-lanceolate—probably narrower in proportion to their length than any others in the genus except *R. makinoi*—with a brown indumentum below. It can grow to 8 or 9ft but does so very slowly. The flowers are bell-shaped, pink in bud opening to white, often with red markings, in April and May. Var. *oreonastes* is a dwarf form with particularly narrow leaves.

R. taliense (H4) grows to about 10ft, tall enough to show the brown indumentum under the leaves. The flowers are bell-shaped, in tight, round trusses, creamy yellow sometimes flushed with pink, with red markings inside, in April and May.

R. wasonii (H4) grows to 6ft or thereabouts and has dark leaves with a bright orange or rusty indumentum below and loose trusses of bell-shaped flowers in May, white, pink or yellow, with crimson spots.

R. wasonii s. Taliense, ss. Wasonii

Thomsonii Series (e)

This is a very important series for the gardener. Most of the series have a characteristic look about the leaves; they never have an indumentum and are usually rounded at both ends, usually shorter than those of the Fortunei series.

R. callimorphum (H4) is a shrub up to 9ft with orbicular, dark green, glossy leaves. The flowers are rose-pink and bell-shaped, opening from April to June. It is a lovely plant and not grown as much as one would expect.

R. caloxanthum (H3–4) grows to about 6ft and again has orbicular leaves, dark above and light below. The flowers are bell-shaped, freely borne, orange in bud opening to yellow, sometimes tinged with pink, in April and May.

R. campylocarpum (H3–4) is one of the best yellow-flowered rhododendrons. The leaves are oblong, the flowers are large and bell-shaped, in loose trusses, opening in April and May. There are two forms, the one makes a bushy shrub, the other is taller and open-growing with orange buds, called var. *elatum*. This species has been used a lot in hybridization to produce yellow-flowered offspring.

R. cerasinum (H4) is not often seen, but is well worth a place in a garden, especially in one form which has white flowers banded with red along the rim of the petals. Other forms have plain red flowers. The flowers are campanulate and pendulous, in May. It grows to about 12ft.

R. litiense (H4) is similar to the better known *R. wardii*. It can grow to 12ft, although it is often smaller, and has trusses of saucer-shaped yellow flowers. The leaves are oblong, glaucous below and very blue when young.

R. souliei (H4) is an outstanding species, unusual in preferring the drier eastern climate to the mild, damp west. The leaves are almost round, with a very blue tinge when young. The flowers are saucer-shaped, white to rose pink, 2in or more in diameter, in graceful trusses, in May. It can reach 12ft.

R. stewartianum (H4) makes a small, graceful bush up to 7 or 8ft. The flower colour is variable in the extreme—white, pale or deep pink, yellow or crimson, but they open in March and so are always at risk from frost.

R. litiense s. Thomsonii, ss. Souliei

R. thomsonii (H4) is one of the best known and best loved of all the rhododendron species, and with justification. It makes a bush or small tree, with an open habit, up to about 20ft, with smooth, peeling reddish-brown bark and almost round leaves that are a vivid blue-green when young. The bell-shaped flowers are in trusses of up to 10, towards the end of April, and are blood-red and long-lasting. A warning is necessary, however. There are forms with paler flowers, var. *candelabrum* and var. *pallidiflorum*, which are not at all attractive, and these are sold as *R. thomsonii*—which of course they are, but not what people expect. A plant that I bought from a perfectly reputable nursery, turned out, when it flowered four years later, to be one of these forms, with deep pink buds that fade to a dreary flesh colour.

R. wardii (H4) is possibly the best yellow-flowered rhododendron that can be grown in most gardens. It is a variable species, different forms can be from 3 to 20ft tall, and they also vary in the size of flower and the intensity of colour, but almost all are good. The flowers open in May and are bowl-shaped, in loose trusses. The leaves are usually almost round but can be oblong, glossy dark green above and whitish below.

R. williamsianum (H3–4) is a very attractive species, unusual in this series in being more or less a dwarf. It has small, round leaves and bronze new growth that appears at the same time as the pink, bell-shaped flowers. This is in early April, and in cold districts both flowers and new growth may be frosted. If the new growth is damaged, more will come later, but the plant will only flower sparsely the following year, if at all. While *R. williamsianum* usually only grows to about 3ft, I have seen it reach 5 or 6ft, especially if drawn up by trees. It has been used a lot in hybridization, transmitting its neat round leaves and campanulate flowers to most of its offspring.

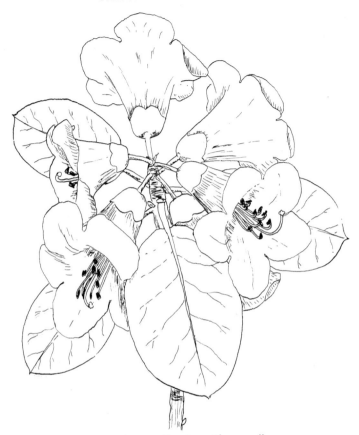

R. thomsonii s. & ss. Thomsonii

Trichocladum Series (l)
This is not a very inspiring series and is little grown, except
for *R. lepidostylum*.
R. lepidostylum (H4) is grown almost entirely as a foliage plant,
and as such, is worth a place in any garden. It forms a dense
little bush about 3ft high with furry, blue-green leaves. The
flowers are smallish and yellow, in May and June; not unat-
tractive but not showy and often hidden by the leaves.

R. trichocladum has flat, pale yellow flowers, with the pedicels sparsely covered with long, white hairs. The deciduous leaves are pale green, almost like those of a Hypericum. It grows to about 4ft and flowers in May.

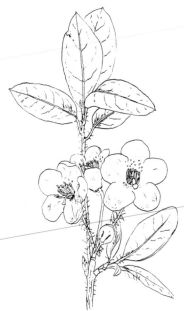

R. trichocladum s. Trichocladum

Triflorum Series (l)

The species of this series are usually easily recognizable, with willowy leaves and wide open, slightly irregular flowers. Although most are tallish, they are upright rather than spreading and do not take up much space. Several of the species are very much like one another. It is a large series, and I will only mention some of the more commonly grown species.

166

R. ambiguum (H4) is a plant where, true to its name, there seems to be some disagreement as to its height—the *RHS Handbook* says 18ft, and 'The Species of Rhododendron' says 5ft. It is not a showy species, with pale yellow flowers in April and May.

R. augustinii (H3–4) is one of the most important species in this series. It forms a shrub up to about 15ft with the typical elegant Triflorum shape and form. In its best forms, the flowers are a luminous, violet blue, but not only are there different colour forms (with, as so often happens, the most desirable being the most tender) but the colour of any one plant seems to vary slightly from year to year, presumably influenced in some way by the weather. The soil, too, appears to have some effect. This is a very free-flowering species,

R. augustinii s. Triflorum, ss. Augustinii

doing so in April and May. The plant that used to be called *R. chasmanthum* is now *R. augustinii* var. *chasmanthum*, and crossed with the type, this has given the 'hybrid' Electra.

R. concinnum (H4) is a shrub of about 10ft with pink to purple flowers in April and May. Var. *pseudoyanthinum* has ruby red flowers.

R. davidsonianum (H3–4) is a leggy plant growing up to 10ft, with flowers of a good, clear pink, often spotted with red, in April and May.

R. hanceanum (H4) grows only to about 4ft, and in the form most commonly grown, var. *nanum*, only to 6in. It is an attractive little plant with bronze new growth and cream or yellow flowers in April.

R. keiskei (H3–4) is another dwarf, unusual in this series, usually growing to only 2ft although I believe there is a taller form, up to about 8ft. The flowers open from March to May and are yellow, but very flimsy in texture. Although it is given H3–4 in the handbook, Leach says that it is the only yellow-flowered rhododendron hardy in the north-east United States, the taller form in particular being hardy as far north as New York.

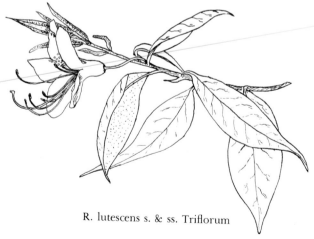

R. lutescens s. & ss. Triflorum

R. lutescens (H3–4) is a graceful plant whose disadvantage is that it starts to flower in February. The flowers tend to keep opening until April, which means that they will not all be frosted; on the other hand, it never makes a great show. The flowers are yellow, in groups of 1–6, both terminal and in the leaf axils. The willowy leaves are bronze in the new growth, which gives a pleasant effect with the yellow flowers, and turn reddish-brown again in autumn.

R. polylepis (H4) has purple flowers in April and grows to about 12ft.

R. rigidum (H4) grows to about 7ft and has smallish pink, white or lavender flowers in clusters of 3–6 in March and April.

R. triflorum (H4) is less striking than some in the series, but has an asset in its red, peeling bark. The flowers are pale yellow, tinged with green or pink. 'Ward's Mahogany Triflorum' has a reddish brown blotch. It flowers in May and grows to about 10ft.

R. yunnanense is a species that will thrive and flower freely even where conditions are not ideal for most rhododendrons, such as a very exposed situation. Some forms are semi-deciduous and in some, the leaves turn bronze in autumn and remain on the branches over winter. The flowers may be white, pink or mauve and are usually spotted with red. Var. *chartophyllum* has white flowers, and is sometimes almost completely deciduous. It flowers in May, very freely.

R. zaleucum (H3–4) has pink, lilac or rarely yellow flowers in April, but the distinctive thing about it (apart from its name) is the white lower surface of the leaves, which contrasts effectively with the dark upper surface. It grows up to about 20ft, but is less hardy than the other species mentioned.

Uniflorum Series (l)
This is another or the really dwarf series.

R. zaleucum is one of the less commonly grown members of the useful *Triflorum* series. It shows the typical wide-open flowers and willowy leaves.

R. imperator (H3–4) is an excellent rock garden plant, rarely growing more than 1ft high, with relatively large, funnel-shaped flowers borne singly or in pairs above the foliage in April and May. The colour varies from pinkish purple to reddish purple, the deeper shades being the more attractive.

R. ludlowii (H3–4) also grows to about 1ft and has small leaves with wavy margins. The flat flowers are about 1in in diameter and yellow, spotted with red, in April and May.

R. pemakoense (H3–4) is very easily grown and so free-flowering that one hopes each year (usually in vain) that it will escape being frosted. In gardens as wide apart as the west of Scotland and Surrey, this has always been the rhododendron whose flowers are most liable to be frosted, even when earlier species, such as *R. moupinense*, escape. It flowers in March and April and once the buds have started to swell they are susceptible to the slightest frost and should, I suppose,

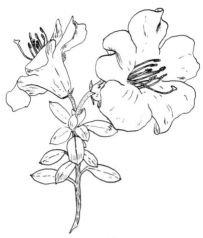

R. pemakoense s. Uniflorum

be covered nightly as a matter of course. The plant itself seems very hardy (I assume from its rating that some forms are less so) and forms a dense, bright green mound about 9in high that spreads by suckering. The flowers are funnel-shaped, about 2in long, lilac or pink.

R. pumilum (H4) is a charming plant but not really a 'good doer', as it tends to languish for no discernible reason. The flowers are little pink bells, opening in May and June. It does not grow more than 1ft tall.

R. uniflorum (H4) is very similar to *R. pemakoense*, but for some reason is less widely grown, although the flowers are deeper in colour and it flowers later, in April and May, both of which should be an advantage.

Virgatum Series (l)
This contains only 2 species, although *R. racemosum* used to be placed here. The flowers are axillary.

R. virgatum (H2–3) grows in a rather leggy way to about 6ft and has pink or white tubular-campanulate flowers in April and May. In spite of its rating, it grows in Edinburgh. *R. oleifolium* (H3) is very similar.

171

CHAPTER 9

Hybrid Rhododendrons

There has, in the past, been too much indiscriminate hybridization, and too many nondescript plants have been put on the market and are still available. The 'hardy hybrids' have a historical interest, and have a place in some very cold gardens and certainly in the north-east United States and continental Europe. They are still far too widely grown, however, in many gardens where good modern hybrids would look more attractive and be more suitable as regards size.

In spite of the vast number of hybrids that exists, there are many species and indeed whole series, that do not seem to have been used at all. In part II of the *Rhododendron Handbook*, almost 200 species are mentioned as having been used in crosses, while over 500 species are listed in Part I as being in general cultivation. One species alone, *R. griersonianum*, is listed as a parent of 136 crosses.

Anyone who wants to start breeding rhododendrons ought to have some definite aim in view, such as improving the colour or size of flowers of a particular type; developing hardier or later flowering forms; achieving dwarfer and more compact types and so on. Haphazard crossing is unlikely to lead to anything exciting. What would be most useful of all would be the breeding of plants which would extend the range of conditions under which the genus could be grown—drought resistant and lime-tolerant, for example.

I have already mentioned that the lepidote and elepidote species have rarely been known to cross. The colours found in the two groups are different—there is no scarlet in the lepidote series, while they alone have 'blue' or violet flowers. In fact, there is no real blue in rhododendrons; the nearest approaches are probably the luminous violet-blue of the best forms of *R. augustinii* and the near royal blue of *R. scintillans*, but both of these are far from the colour of a gentian or a lithospermum. There are two distinct factors responsible for flower colour and each is inherited separately. There are soluble colours dissolved in the sap—yellow and white flavanols and red and blue anthocyanins—and insoluble pigments contained in small bodies called plastids; these give white and yellow.

Certain species of rhododendron are likely to be incompatible due to having different chromosome numbers, even assuming they belong to the same group, either lepidote or elepidote. The basic chromosome number for the genus is 13; most species are diploid, that is they have 26 chromosomes (13 pairs), but *R. canadense* and *R. calendulaceum*, for example, are tetraploid (52 chromosomes) and *R. cinnabarinum* and *R. yunnanense* hexaploid (78 chromosomes).

If one wants to make a cross, the stamens of the flower selected as seed parent should be removed, and when its stigma appears sticky, pollen from the flower selected as the pollen parent should be brushed on to it. It is safest then to enclose the flower in some sort of bag until it has withered to avoid the risk of a second pollination by bees. Once the pod shows signs of swelling, the bag can be removed and the flower in question must be clearly labelled, as the pod will not be ready for picking before October. At least for some species, the characteristics that are likely to be passed on when they are used as parents, are now fairly well known. For example *R. forrestii* usually passes on its dwarf stature and red colour; *R. williamsianum* its rounded leaves and the shape of its bell-shaped flowers; *R. griersonianum* its long-tubed flower shape, pointed bud scales and something of its red colour.

Hybrids often seem to be hardier than either parent, and the flowering time is usually intermediate between that of the parents. But even those with the most experience cannot predict exactly how a cross will turn out, which is doubtless the fascination that breeding rhododendrons holds for many people. In fact, the same parents crossed can give results of very different quality on different occasions. The product of any cross between the same two parents is called a grex. A clone is all the offspring, vegetatively produced, of any one plant, which may be either a species or a hybrid. This is the only way in which a particularly good form can be reproduced exactly, as even self-pollinated seed will show some variation. Thus we have *R × loderi* 'King George', 'Venus', and many others, each being a different clone of the basic cross.

A lot of breeding in the past few decades has been done at some of the great private gardens, such as Bodnant, Leonardslee, Exbury, Tower Court and Caerhays. Most of the nurseries listed at the end of the book have gone in for hybridization, too. Some have specialized in one way or another, for example Glendoick has produced mainly dwarf hybrids, outstanding examples being Chikor and Ptarmigan, while Knap Hill has largely specialized in deciduous azaleas. The RHS gardens at Wisley and the Savill Garden in Windsor Great Park have also produced some fine hybrids.

It is difficult to know how to deal in an organized way with the descriptions of hybrid rhododendrons; they do not fall into even such reasonably neat categories as do the hybrid azaleas. Simply for convenience, I propose to divide them into four classes. First, the hardy hybrids, most of which date back to the last century. They are wind-, cold- and often sun-resistant, and are large and bulky looking plants—usually too large for the average garden of today. They have big flowers in showy trusses and usually flower freely year after year, but the foliage is almost always undistinguished and the bushes tend to form shapeless mounds. Planted en masse, these hybrids give a very turgid effect, but the occasional one, carefully placed in a garden amongst other genera, can give an effective show of colour in the flowering season, and can be useful as a windbreak for more choice varieties. The colour range is limited—white, pink, mauve, red and purple. There are few clear yellows, and the reds are always on the blue side, hinting at magenta if not actually achieving it.

I am sure that the reason these types are still so widely grown in places where they need not be, is simply that they are readily available. In *Rhododendron in the North*, published by the Northern Horticultural Society, the authors found in their survey that the list of species found to be the most popular corresponded pretty closely with those offered by the greatest number of nurserymen (excluding rhododendron specialists) in the area. I feel this connection must hold even more strongly for the hardy hybrids, which are stocked by almost every nursery and garden centre in the country.

It is impossible to give anything like a comprehensive list of all the varieties that are available, I have just made what I hope is a fairly representative selection. 'Small' in this context means under 5ft.

The second group is what is sometimes called the 'woodland hybrids' but might be better called tall 'modern' hybrids. Again, these are mostly fairly large plants and most need some shelter. Some are extremely beautiful, however, and many gardens might find a place for one or two of them.

Thirdly, there are compact hybrids, which grow perhaps 4 or 5ft tall and are good-tempered in any reasonable situation, and finally, the dwarf hybrids, which are far fewer than might be expected, but seem to be gaining both in popularity and numbers. The last two of these groups are by far the most important for most gardens.

FCC—1st Class Certificate
AM—Award of Merit } Awards given by the RHS
AGM—Award of Garden Merit

THE HARDY HYBRIDS

Most of these are the result of involved crossing, in many the parentage is unknown.

A. Bedford—(*ponticum* ×)—AM 1936. H4. Tall, vigorous, lavender with a dark eye. May.

Album elegans—(*catawbiense* ×)—H4. Large, very hardy, good windbreak. Lavender buds, opening paler. May.

Alice—(*griffithianum* ×)—AM 1910. H4. Tall, less hardy than some. Deep pink buds, opening paler. May.

Ascot Brilliant. Tall, deep red. H4. Raised in 1861 and possibly, although parentage is unknown, one of earliest *R. thomsonii* hybrids. April/May.

Bagshot Ruby—(*thomsonii* × John Waterer)—AM 1916. H4. Medium size, crimson. May. Hardy to − 10°C, and heat resistant.

Betty Wormald—(George Hardy ×)—AM 1935, FCC 1964, AGM 1968. H4. Tall. Large pink flowers, spotted crimson. May. Does well in southern U.S.A. if given shade.

Blue Danube—(*discolor* × Purple Splendour). H4. Medium size but fast growing. Lavender blue, May.

Blue Peter. AM 1935, FCC 1958, AGM 1968. H4. Medium size, spreading. Lavender blue, frilly, with dark blotch. May. Heat resistant.

Boule de Neige—*R. caucasicum* × *R. catawbiense* hybrid. H4. Compact but vigorous, white. An old variety still useful in the USA because of its great hardiness—to −25°C.

Britannia—(Queen Wilhelmina × Stanley Davies)—AM 1921, FCC 1937, AGM 1968. H4. Compact, large trusses of frilly crimson flowers. Yellow-green foliage. May/June. Does well in southern USA.

Cetewayo. AM 1959. H4. Medium size, dark purplish red, May.

Christmas Cheer—(*caucasicum* ×). H4. Smallish, pale pink, March. Will stand a lot of sun.

Countess of Athlone—(*catawbiense grandiflorum* × Geoffrey Millais). H4. Medium size, lilac. April/May. Fairly sun-tolerant.

Countess of Derby—(Pink Pearl × Cynthia)—AM 1930. H4. Large, robust, rose pink. May.

Cunningham's Sulphur. H4. May not be a hybrid but a form of *R. caucasicum*. Smallish, compact, pale yellow. April.

Cunningham's White. H4. Large, vigorous, white. May.

Cynthia (*catawbiense* × *griffithianum*) AGM 1968. H4. Large and vigorous. Catalogues describe the colour as 'rosy crimson' but some would call it magenta. Heat resistant.

Doncaster—(*arboreum* ×). H4. Smallish, slow-growing, bluish-red. May. Fairly heat tolerant.

Duchess of Connaught. H4. Large, spreading, white with yellow blotch. May/June.

Everestianum—(*catawbiense* ×). H4. Medium; frilly lilac-pink flowers. May/June.

Fatsuosum Flore Pleno—(probably *catawbiense* × *ponticum*). AGM 1928. H4. Tall, robust, large semi-double, blue-mauve flowers. May/June. Will stand full exposure.

Furnival's Daughter. FCC 1961. H4. Large, bright pink with dark blotch. April/May.

Goldfort—(Goldsworth Yellow × *fortunei*). H4. Large, creamy yellow with pink flush. May.

Goldsworth Crimson—(*griffithianum* × Doncaster)—AM 1960. H4. Tall, crimson. April.

Goldsworth Yellow—(*caucasicum* × *campylocarpum*). AM 1925 and 34. H4. Small to medium, apricot buds, opening yellow. May.

Gomer Waterer—(*catawbiense* ×). AM 1906, AGM 1968. H4. Large, vigorous, lilac buds opening white; glossy dark foliage, good windbreak. May/June. Heat and sun tolerant.

Halopeanum—(*griffithianum* × *maximum*). H4. Sometimes known as 'White Pearl', and is rather like a paler Pink Pearl. Large. May.

Helene Schiffner. FCC 1893. H4. Pure white, loose trusses of smallish flowers, medium grower. May.

John Walter—(*arboreum* × *catawbiense*). H4. Medium, crimson, June.

John Waterer. H4. Medium—tall, dark red, very hardy. May.

Kluis Sensation—(Britannia ×). H4. Compact, similar to Britannia but with darker flowers and better foliage. June.

Kluis Triumph—(*griffithianum* ×). H4. Small, dark red with black spots. May/June.

Lady Clementine Mitford—(*maximum* ×). H4. Medium, peach pink flowers; good foliage, silvery when young. June. Fairly heat resistant.

Lady de Rothschild—(*griffithianum* × Sappho). Medium, white spotted red. June.

Lady Eleanor Cathcart—(*arboreum* × *maximum*). H4. Tall, vigorous, deep pink with dark eye. June.

Gomer Waterer

Lady Longman—(Cynthia × Lady Eleanor Cathcart). H4.
 Similar to the last, with larger trusses. June.
Lord Roberts. H4. Tall, very hardy, dark red with black
 spots. June.·

Lowinsky's White. Tall, white flowers from pink buds. June.

Marchioness of Lansdowne—(*maximum* ×). H4. Medium; rose pink with dark eye. June.

Mars—(*griffithianum* ×). AM 1928, FCC 1935. H4. Medium; dark red. May. Heat resistant if given mid-day shade.

Moser's Maroon. AM 1932. H4. Large; dark maroon flowers; foliage red in new growth. June. Does well in sun.

Mother of Pearl—(Pink Pearl ×, or might be sport from Pink Pearl) AM 1930, AGM 1968. H4. Similar to PP, not quite so large; paler pink flowers. May.

Mount Everest. AM 1953, FCC 1958. H4. Tall, white with brown spots. April.

Mrs A. T. de la Mare—(Halopeanum × Sir Charles Butler). AM 1958, AGM 1968. H4. Large, vigorous, good foliage; scented white flowers with green blotch, from pink buds. Better with some shelter. May.

Mrs Charles Pearson—(*catawbiense grandiflorum* × Coombe Royal). AM 1933, FCC 1955. H4. Tall; lavender spotted brown. May.

Mrs Davies Evans—AM 1958. H4. Compact grower; frilly lilac flowers and good dark foliage.

Mrs Furnival—(*caucasicum* hybrid × *griffithianum* hybrid). FCC 1948, AGM 1968. H4. Large; soft pink with brown eye. June.

Mrs G. W. Leak—(Chevalier Felix de Sauvage × Coombe Royal). FCC 1934, AGM 1968. H4. Medium to tall, pink with brown blotch. May.

Mrs Lindsay Smith—(George Hardy × Duchess of Edinburgh). AM 1933. H4. Tall, vigorous, white flowers flushed pink; dark, deeply veined foliage. May/June.

Mrs R. S. Holford. H4. Tall, vigorous, frilly salmon pink flowers (unusual in a hardy hybrid). June.

Mrs T. H. Lowinsky. AM 1919. H4. Large, vigorous, pink

'Mrs Furnival' is a splendid example of a dark-eyed 'hardy hybrid'. The flowers are pink.

buds opening white with orange blotch. June. Fairly heat tolerant.

Nobleanum—(*arboreum* × *caucasicum*). AGM 1926. H4. The earliest of these to flower, January/March. Medium sized, rose-crimson. Var. *album* is white; var. *venustum* is pink and even earlier than the type.

Old Port—(*catawbiense* ×). H4. Plum red, medium sized, very hardy. June.

Peter Koster—(Doncaster × George Hardy). AM 1946. H4. Medium; bright pink, June.

Picotee. H4. Medium; white flowers edged pink. May.

Pink Pearl—(*Broughtonii* × George Hardy). AM 1897, FCC 1900. H4. The best known of all hybrid rhododendrons. Tall, with huge trusses of frilly pink flowers. Blowsy but undeniably showy. May. Does well in southern USA.

Purple Splendour—(*ponticum* ×). AM 1931, AGM 1968. H4. Medium; deep purple with black eye. June. Fairly heat resistant.

Royal Purple. H4. Deep purple with yellow eye; large. June.

Sappho. AGM 1968. H4. A very old variety, still widely grown. White with a purple blotch. Tall. May.

Sigismund Rucker. FCC 1872. H4. Medium; magenta with dark blotch; very hardy. May/June.

Susan—(*campanulatum* × *fortunei*). AM 1930, FCC 1950, AGM 1968. Tall, good foliage, lavender blue. May.

The Bride. FCC 1871. H4. An old variety, medium sized, lavender buds opening to white flowers with green eye. May/June. Fairly heat tolerant.

The term 'hardy hybrid' is possibly an unfortunate one, in that it implies that other hybrids are not hardy, which is by no means so. These other hybrids are a heterogeneous collection, ranging from the large and opulent 'Loderi' grex, to the elegant bells of 'Lady Chamberlain'.

TALL MODERN HYBRIDS

Adelaide—(Aurora × *thomsonii*), AM 1935. H3. Tall, red flowers, May.

Akbar—(*Loderi* 'King George' × *discolor*), AM 1952. Tall, pink flowers, May.

Aladdin—(*griersonianum* × *auriculatum*), AM 1935. H4. July flowering, takes size from *R. auriculatum*. Bright rose pink flowers. Needs shelter, but is tolerant of heat.

Albatross—(*Loderi* × *discolor*) AM 1934 & 53, AGM 1968. H4. Tall; pink buds opening to frilly white flowers, heavily scented; long, elegant bright green leaves. June.

Angelo—(*discolor* × *griffithianum*). AM 1935. H3 but in America rated hardy to −5°C. Similar to the last, but even larger and later to flower.

Avalanche—(*calophytum* × *Loderi*), AM 1934 (to pink form) FCC 1938 (to white form). H3. Pink or white flowers, not too hardy.

Avocet—(*discolor* × *fortunei*). Very large, scented white flowers in June.

Azor—(*discolor* × *griersonianum*), AM 1933. H4. Large shrub or small tree, with pink flowers in July.

Barclayi—(Glory of Penjerrick × *thomsonii*), AM 1921 to clone 'Robert Fox'. H3. Blood red flowers, dark foliage, not for colder gardens. April.

Beau Brummel—(*eriogynum* × Essex Scarlet). AM 1938. Waxy scarlet flowers, spotted with black in July.

Bibiani—(*arboreum* × Moser's Maroon), AM 1934. H4. Deep red flowers with black eye in April, makes large bush rather than a tree.

Biskra—(*ambiguum* × *cinnabarinum*), var. *roylei*. AM 1940. H3. This has the *R. cinnabarinum* habit, but the flowers are less tubular, vermilian red, in May.

Billy Budd—(*elliottii* × May Day), AM 1957. H3. A striking plant with large trusses of dark red flowers in May.

Boddaertianum—(*arboreum* × *campanulatum*). H4. Long narrow leaves, pink buds opening to white flowers with dark spots. April.

Bonito—(*discolor* × Luscombei), AM 1934. H4. Very large, pink, scented flowers, quick growing and hardy. July.

Bustard—(*auriculatum* × Penjerrick). H3. Cream flowers with dark eyes, not for cold gardens. July.

Carex—*irroratum* × *fargesii*, AM 1932. H3. Bell-shaped, pale pink flowers, spotted red, in April.

Carita—(Naomi × *campylocarpum*), AM 1945. H4. Neat foliage, peach-pink buds opening to yellow flowers in April, well set off by purplish stalks. A lovely shrub, that can grow to about 15ft. There are cream and pink forms.

China—(*wightii* × *fortunei*), AM 1940 and 48. H4. Creamy flowers with red throat, in May. Rather spreading.

Cinnkeys—(*cinnabarinum* × *keysii*), AM 1935. H4. Tall and upright, with tubular yellow flowers tipped with red, in May.

Cornish Cross—(*griffithianum* × *thomsonii*). H3. Large, opulent crimson-pink flowers in March and April. Pinky-brown, peeling bark. Spectacular, but only for warm districts.

Cornubia—(*arboreum* × *Shilsonii*), AM 1912. H3. Tall and vigorous, blood red trusses in March and April.

Crest—see Hawk.

Damask—(*eriogynum* × *Loderi*), AM 1932. Large, deep pink flowers in May and June.

Dr Stocker—(*caucasicum* × *griffithianum*), AM 1900. H3. Cream flowers with a red throat in large trusses. April.

Electra—(*augustinii* × *augustinii* var. *chasmanthum*). H3. Startlingly beautiful in full flower but can be temperamental. Vivid violet blue flowers in May.

Firebird—(*griersonianum* × Norman Shaw). H4. Bright red flowers in June.

Fusilier—(*elliottii* × *griersonianum*), AM 1938, FCC 1942. H3. Vivid scarlet, dark-spotted flowers in June.

Gill's Crimson (*griffithianum* ×). H3. Tall but compact, large scarlet flowers in April.

Gladys—(campylocarpum × fortunei), AM 1926, AM 1950 to clone 'Rose'. H4. Yellow buds opening to cream flowers, spotted purple, in May.

Grenadier—(*elliottii* × Moser's Maroon). H3. Tall and vigorous with large trusses of dark red flowers in July.

Hawk—(Lady Bessborough × *wardii*). AM 1949. H3. There are

several forms of this fine cross, all yellow, medium to tall, May flowering. Some of the clones are; Crest (FCC 1953)—lemon yellow; Kestrel; Merlin; Jervis Bay (AM 1951)—the tallest, with a red blotch.

Idealist—(Naomi × *wardii*), AM 1945. H4. Tall, but neat. Pinkish orange buds opening to creamy-yellow flowers in May.

Inamorata (*wardii* × *discolor*), AM 1950. H4. Cream flowers, flushed yellow, with purple stalks, in June and July.

Jalisco—(Dido × Lady Bessborough). H4. Again there are several clones, all of varying shades of yellow, some with a red blotch. Eclipse (AM 1948); Elect, (AM 1948); Goshawk (FCC 1954).

Jocelyne—(*calophytum* × *lacteum*), AM 1954, FCC 1956. Large trusses of cream flowers with a dark blotch, fine foliage. April/May.

Josephine—(Ayah × *wardii*). Pink buds opening to cream flowers in July.

Kewense—(*fortunei* × *griffithianum*). H3. The same cross as gave *Loderi*; not so large, but hardier. Scented pale pink flowers in May.

Kilimanjaro—(Dusky Maid × *elliottii*), AM 1947. H3. Rich red flowers in May.

Ladybird—(Corona × *discolor*), AM 1933. H4. Trusses of deep pink flowers with a dark eye, in July. Large and vigorous.

Lady Berry—(Rosy Bell × Royal Flush), AM 1933, FCC 1949. H3. Smaller than most of this group, with beautiful long-tubed flowers, yellow flushed with salmon, in May. Very much a plant for mild gardens.

Lady Bessborough (*campylocarpum* × *discolor*), FCC 1933. H4. Loose trusses of creamy yellow flowers opening from pink buds in May. Roberte (FCC 1936) is a clone with salmon flowers, gradually turning yellow.

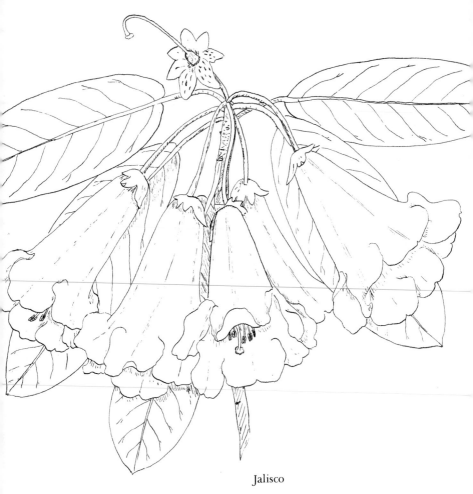

Jalisco

Lady Chamberlain—(*cinnabarinum* var. *roylei* × Royal Flush).
H3. One of the most beautiful of all hybrids; similar
to *R. cinnabarinum*, with long, waxy, pendant flowers, but
these are larger. There are many forms, some of which
are: FCC form (1931)—orange salmon; Exbury form—
yellow-orange; Gleam—yellow-orange tipped with red;

186

Golden Queen (FCC 1947)—golden yellow; Salmon Trout—salmon.

Lady Rosebery—(*cinnabarinum* var. *roylei* × Royal Flush pink form), FCC 1932. H3. Similar to the last, but the different forms have flowers of varying shades of pink, eg Dalmeny; Pink Dawn; Pink Delight. This and the last both flower in May.

Lavender Girl—(*fortunei* × Lady Grey Egerton), AM 1950, FCC 1967, AGM 1968. H4. Pale lavender, free-flowering, May/June. Will stand full exposure.

Leonore—(*auriculatum* × *kyawi*), AM 1948. Large and spreading, with loose trusses of pink flowers in July.

Letty Edwards—(*campylocarpum* var. *elatum* × *fortunei*), FCC 1948, AGM 1968. H4. Pink buds opening to yellow flowers in May; a very attractive plant.

Lionel's Triumph—(*lacteum* × Naomi), AM 1954. H3. A splendid yellow with a red blotch in April and May.

Lodauric—(*auriculatum* × *Loderi*), AM 1958. H4. Scented white flowers with a green eye; bronze new growth. Hardier than *Loderi*.

Loderi—(*fortunei* × *griffithianum*). H3. Large and vigorous; enormous frilly flowers, heavily scented, pink in bud, in most forms opening white but in some, staying pink. Helen; Pink Diamond (FCC 1914, AGM 1968); Sir Joseph Hooker and Venus (AGM 1968) are pink. King George (AM 1968, AGM 1968): Titan and White Diamond (FCC 1914) are white. No less than 23 clones are listed in the Studbook. They flower in May, and all must have wind shelter.

Loder's White—(*arboreum album* × *griffithianum*), AGM 1931. H3. Elongated white trusses opening from pink buds. Not so sumptuous as Loderi, but possibly more refined.

Lord Swaythling—AM 1926, 1954. H3. Large and vigorous; frilly deep pink flowers profusely borne in April.

Mariloo—(Dr Stocker × *lacteum*), AM 1950. H3. A vigorous grower with huge yellow flowers, in April. Needs wind-shelter.

Naomi—(Aurora × *fortunei*), AM 1935. H4. Rounded foliage with purple stalks, like *R. fortunei*. Large trusses of scented flowers, which vary from lilac to pink to salmon, depending on form. The AM form is lilac pink; Carissima is salmon pink; Exbury form is pinkish-yellow; Nautilus (AM 1938) is pink flushed orange and Stella Maris (FCC 1939) is pinkish buff. Does well in southern states of USA.

Oreocinn—(*oreotrephes* × *cinnabarinum*). H4. Very free flowering; pink flowers with a yellow flush in May.

Penelope—(*griersonianum* × *Dragonfly*). Good foliage, scarlet flowers in June.

Penjerrick—(*campylocarpum* var. *elatum* × *griffithianum*) AM 1923. H3. Probably competes with the Ladies Chamberlain, Rosebery and Berry as being the most beautiful of all hybrids. Makes a small tree with coppery bark and good, bright green foliage with pink bracts on the new growth. Loose trusses of bell-shaped flowers, in April and May, which may be cream, yellow or pink. Should have wind shelter.

Pilgrim—(*fortunei* × Gill's Triumph), AM 1926. H4. Rounded, *fortunei*-like foliage, large trusses of pink flowers.

Polar Bear—(*auriculatum* × *diaprepes*), FCC 1946. H3. Makes a large, spreading tree up to 40ft tall, with good foliage and large trusses of scented white flowers July and August.

Pyrex—(*facetum* × *haematodes*). Brilliant scarlet flowers in May.

Queen Souriya—(*campylocarpum* hybrid × *fortunei*). AM 1957. H4. Yellowish flowers edged with lilac pink, in May.

Red Admiral (*arboreum* × *thomsonii*). H4. Blood red flowers in March and April.

'Lord Swaythling' is a free-flowering hybrid that needs some shelter, with pink, frilly flowers.

Repose—(*discolor* × *lacteum*), AM 1956. H4. Large, creamy yellow flowers in May.

Revlon—(*cinnabarinum* var. *roylei* × Lady Chamberlain), AM 1957. Good, glaucous foliage, carmine flowers like those of Lady Chamberlain.

Romany Chai—(Moser's Maroon × *griersonianum*), AM 1932. Crimson flowers spotted with black in July and August, dark foliage. Hardier than some of the *R. griersonianum* hybrids, but less distinguished than most of them.

Romany Chal—(*eriogynum* × Moser's Maroon), AM 1932, FCC 1937. H3. Waxy, blood red flowers with brown spots, in July and August. These last two hybrids are useful for their late flowering time.

Rosabel—(*griersonianum* × Pink Shell), AM 1936. H3. Large, pale pink flowers.

Rosy Morn—(*Loderi* × *souliei*), AM 1931. Pink, saucer-shaped flowers, opening paler, in June. Rounded foliage.

Royal Blood—(*elliottii* × Rubens), AM 1954. Large trusses of up to 40 dark red flowers, in May.

Royal Flush—(*cinnabarinum* × *maddenii*). H3. Beautiful but rather tender. Foliage like *R. cinnabarinum*; trumpet-shaped pink or yellow flowers in May.

Shilsonii—(*barbatum* × *thomsonii*), AM 1900. H3. Splendid, brilliant red flowers in March, good reddish-brown bark. Not for cold areas.

Sir Frederick Moore—(*discolor* × St Keverne), AM 1937. H4. Large, frilly scented pink flowers in June.

Sir Charles Lemon—(*arboreum* ×). Splendid foliage, dark above, bright orange-brown below. Creamy flowers in April.

Trewithen Orange—(*concatens* × Full House), FCC 1950. H4. Tubular, salmon-orange flowers; very handsome.

Unique—(*campylocarpum* ×), AM 1934, FCC 1935. H4. Pink buds opening to creamy flowers with red stalks, in April.

Yunncinn—(*yunnanense* × *cinnabarinum*). Tubular campanulate lilac flowers. The clone 'Youthful Sin' received an AM in 1960.

Yvonne—(Aurora × *griffithianum*). H3. Not unlike Loderi, but with smaller, neater flowers. Opalene (AM 1931) is mauve, fading to cream; Pride (AM 1948) is cream, with a dark eye. May.

Unique

COMPACT HYBRIDS

The next group of hybrids includes those that are not dwarfs, but would not be expected to grow more than 5 or 6ft tall. Obviously, such divisions are arbitrary; some plants could be fitted into either (i) this group or the previous one (such as the *R. augustinii* hybrids St Breward and St Tudy) or (ii) this group or the dwarfs. There are a number of 'blue' hybrids which tend to look very much alike, mostly crosses of *R. augustinii* with one of the blue or mauve members of the Lapponicum series. They vary in size from small to fairly tall, so will be divided between this group and the next. There are many at Wisley, both in the rock garden and in the approach to Battlestone Hill; all are gay and free flowering, usually in April and early May, with neat, small leaves.

Alison Johnstone—(*concatens* × *yunnanense*), AM 1945. H4. This just gets in here instead of in the 'tall' section, as it can grow to about 6ft, but is neat and compact. It has apricot, azalea-like flowers in May.

Anita—(*campylocarpum* × *griersonianum*). H3. Loose trusses of pink, bell-shaped flowers, in May.

Arthur Osborn—(*sanguineum* var. *didymum* × *griersonianum*) AM 1933. H3. Dark foliage; deep red flowers in June.

Augfast—(*augustinii* × *fastigiatum*). H4. Can grow up to 5ft. Violet blue flowers in April and May.

Azamia—(*augustinii* × *russatum* var. *cantabile*). Medium sized, bright 'blue' flowers in April.

Blue Diamond—(*augustinii* × *Intrifast*), AM 1935, FCC 1939, AGM 1968. H4. One of the best of the *R. augustinii* hybrids. Has a columnar habit up to 5ft or so, very free-flowering, deep violet blue; very hardy. April/May.

Bo-peep—(*lutescens* × *moupinense*), AM 1937. H3. Creamy yellow flowers, bronze new growth. Would not seem very showy later in the season, but flowering in March and early April, it has considerable charm.

Bow Bells—(Corona × *williamsianum*), AM 1935. H4. Virtually all the *R. williamsianum* hybrids have the rounded leaves and campanulate flowers of that parent, and usually a compact, rounded habit. This one has coppery new growth and salmon-pink flowers in May. About 4ft tall.

Brocade—(Vervaenianum × *williamsianum*). H4. Up to 5ft, rather spreading. Large, pink bells in April, opening from darker buds.

Burma Road—(Fabia Tangerine × Romany Chal), AM 1958. Apricot flowers, flushed with pink, in May and June.

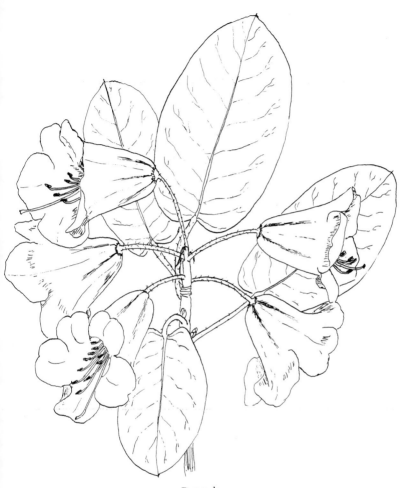

Brocade

Canary—(*caucasicum* × *campylocarpum*). Grows to about 4ft. Yellow flowers in May; very hardy.

Cinzah—(*cinnabarinum* × *xanthocodon*). Hanging, tubular apricot flowers in May.

Comely—(concatens × Lady Chamberlain). Small trusses of yellow flowers in April and May.

Conyan—(*concatens* × *concinnum* var. *pseudoyanthinum*). Hardy and free-flowering, with tubular flowers varying from apricot to salmon to pink.

Coral Reef—(Fabia × Goldsworth Orange), AM 1954. H4. Yellow and apricot flowers, shaded salmon, in May.

Cowslip—(*wardii* × *williamsianum*), AM 1937. H4. Up to 4ft; pink buds opening to creamy yellow bells in April and May.

Crossbill—(*lutescens* × *spinuliferum*). H3. Unusual and interesting looking, with yellow, tubular flowers, tinged with apricot in April.

Dairymaid—(*campylocarpum* ×), AM 1934. H4. Creamy yellow, blotched with red, in April.

Damaris Logan (*campylocarpum* × Dr Stocker), AM 1948. H3. Clear yellow flowers, spotted with red, in May.

David—(Hugh Koster × *neriiflorum*), AM 1957, FCC 1939. H4. Deep blood red flowers in white anthers in May.

Daydream—(Lady Bessborough × *griersonianum*), AM 1940. H3. Hardier than might be expected. Deep pink buds, the flowers fading to creamy yellow as they open. May/June.

Dormouse—(Dawn's Delight × *williamsianum*). H4. Similar to *R. williamsianum* itself, but larger in leaf and flowers. Salmon pink bells in April; grows to 4 or 5ft.

Elizabeth—(*forrestii* var. *repens* × *griersonianum*), AM 1939, FCC 1943. H4. One of the best and most widely grown of the modern hybrids. Compact, growing to 4 or 5ft, with dark foliage and loose trusses of large vermilion, long-tubed flowers in April and May. Hardy and free-flowering, often with a second flush in the autumn. Jenny is a prostrate clone, and looks particularly well trailing down a bank.

Elizabeth

Emasculum—(*ciliatum* × *dauricum*). H4. The same cross as gave the better known *Praecox*. This too has rosy lilac flowers, but is taller and slightly later, in. April. It has no stamens.

Fabia (*dichroanthum* × *griersonianum*), AM 1934. H4. A lovely plant, with loose, elegant trusses of orange flowers in June. There are several clones, which include, Exbury— the tallest, up to 6ft, salmon-orange; Roman Pottery— more spreading, terracotta; Tangerine—tangerine orange, with a petaloid calyx; Tower Court—the small-est, pinkish orange.

Fabia Orange

Fairy Light—(*griersonianum* × Lady Marr). Salmon pink, in June and July.

Fine Feathers—(Cilpinense × *lutescens*). Rather like Bo-peep, with larger leaves. Lemon yellow flowers in early April.

Flamingo—(*griersonianum* × Loder's White). Well-shaped deep pink flowers in elegant trusses. June.

Flashlight (*callimorphum* × *campylocarpum*). H3. Apricot buds opening to yellow flowers in May.

Goblin—(Break of Day × *griersonianum*), AM 1939. H3. Open trusses of orange-red flowers in May.

Golden Cockerel—(May Day × Lascaux). H3. A compact grower, with red buds opening to golden flowers.

Golden Horn—(*dichroanthum* × *elliottii*), AM 1945. H4. Orange-red buds opening to orange flowers, spotted brown, with a double calyx. Persimmon is taller and waxy scarlet, without a double calyx. This is a splendid plant. May.

Golden Orfe—(*concatens* × Lady Chamberlain), AM 1964. Tubular yellow flowers, flushed with orange.

Grayswood Pink—(*venator* × *williamsianum*). Smallish, very hardy, with deep pink bells in May.

Grosclaude—(*haematodes* × *eriogynum*), AM 1945. H4. Waxy red bells with a petalloid calyx in June and July. Dark leaves with a brown indumentum below.

Halcyone—(Lady Bessborough × *souliei*). H4. Pink buds opening to saucer-shaped creamy flowers with a brownish eye, in May. It has pleasant, rounded leaves. Perdita (AM 1948) is pink and yellow, with a purple throat.

Humming Bird—(*haematodes* × *williamsianum*). H3. A very good hybrid; dark leaves with a slight brown indumentum below; waxy crimson-pink bells in May. Makes a rounded mound, about 4ft high. 'Elizabeth Lockhart' is a clone of this, discovered by Professor R. D. Lockhart of Aberdeen, which is unique among rhododendrons in having coloured foliage. In his own words; 'The young foliage of Elizabeth Lockhart is more brilliant than the young leaves of copperbeech; the bells, in loose clusters, are dark red; the under side of the leaf has red veining, but no brown indumentum; a broken twig shows a red centre; the old foliage is brown.' The whole plant gives the impression of being suffused with dark red, it is a most interesting and unusual effect.

Ibex—(*griersonianum* × *pocophorum*), AM 1948. H4. Good dark pointed leaves with a brown indumentum below; vermilion-scarlet flowers in good trusses in April.

Icarus—(A. Gilbert × *dichroanthum* subsp. *herpesticum*), AM 1947. H4. Hanging yellow flowers, flushed with pink, in May and June.

Impi—(*sanguineum* subsp. *didymum* × Moser's Maroon), AM 1945. H4. A compact grower, with deep blood red flowers in June and July.

Iviza—(Bustard × Fabia). Tubular campanulate yellow flowers, in June and July. Philomel is a clone with pink tinge.

Joanita—(*lacteum* × *caloxanthum*). Its R. *lacteum* 'blood' makes it a bit temperamental, but it has lovely daffodil yellow flowers opening from orange buds.

Jutland—(Bellerophon × *elliottii*), AM 1947. H3. Not very hardy, but a good plant where it can be grown, with large, vivid, waxy red flowers in July.

Lady Bowes Lyon—(Pilgrim × *yakusimanum*), AM 1962. Round trusses of pink and white bell-shaped flowers in May. Makes a spreading bush up to about 4ft.

Lascaux—(Fabia × *litiense*), AM 1954. H3. Yellow flowers with a red blotch in May and June.

Maestro—(Barclayi × *williamsianum*), dark red bell-shaped flowers in April.

Mandalay—(*haematodes* × *venator*). Hardy, compact and prolific, with scarlet flowers in May.

Marcia—(*campylocarpum* × Gladys), FCC 1944. H3. Round trusses of yellow flowers opening from orange buds in May.

Margaret Dunn—(*discolor* × Fabia), AM 1946. H4. Loose trusses of apricot bells, yellow in the throat, in June and July.

Matador—(*griersonianum* × *strigillosum*), AM 1945, FCC 1946. H3. Narrow, hairy leaves, lax trusses of long-tubed scarlet flowers in April.

May Day—(*griersonianum* × *haematodes*), AM 1932, AGM 1968. H3. A splendid plant, hardy, compact and free-flowering. Vivid scarlet, tubular-campanulate flowers, good dark foliage with a brown indumentum below.

May Morn—(*beanianum* pink form × May Day), AM 1946. Rosy crimson flowers in April and May; leaves with a brown indumentum below.

Medusa (*griersonianum* × *dichroanthum* subsp. *scyphocalyx*). H3. Bell-shaped orange flowers in May; leaves with a greyish indumentum below.

Mohamet—(*dichroanthum* × Tally Ho), AM 1945. H3. Orange flowers with a pinkish tinge in June.

Moonshine—(Adriaan Koster × *litiense*), AM 1952. H4. Hardy and free-flowering, with bright yellow flowers. There are several named clones, eg Crescent (AM 1960); Supreme (AM 1953).

Mystic—(Barclayi × *williamsianum*). From the same cross as Maestro and similar to it, but with pink flowers, also in April. A lovely plant, but none too hardy.

Nereid—(*dichroanthum* × *neriiflorum*). H3. A compact grower, with loose trusses of salmon pink bell-shaped flowers in May.

Pink Pebble—(*callimorphum* × *williamsianum*). Pink, bell-shaped flowers in May.

Praecox—(*ciliatum* × *dauricum*), AGM 1926. H4. This is an invaluable plant for any garden. It has rosy lilac flowers in February and March, that do not all open at once, so that all are not likely to be frosted. Although small-leaved and lightly built, it can grow to 5 or 6ft. *Praecox* may be evergreen or semi-deciduous, depending on which form of *R. dauricum* was used to make the cross.

Redcap—(*sanguineum* subsp. *didymum* × *eriogynum*). H3. Very dark red; reaches 4ft, so just escapes the dwarf class. 'Townhill' form received an AM in 1945. July.

Remo—(*lutescens* × *valentinianum*). H3. Again, just misses the dwarf class. Bright yellow flowers in April; a cheerful plant, but not for cold gardens.

Renoir—(*yakusimanum* × Pauline), AM 1961. Pink and white flowers, spotted red, in May. Compact, to about 4ft.

Rosalind—(*fargesii* × *thomsonii*), AM 1938. This one is just verging on the tall class. Good foliage, and deep pink bells in April and May.

Rozamarie—(?Penjerrick × *wardii*). Clear yellow bell-shaped flowers in May.

St Breward—(*augustinii* × *impeditum*), FCC 1962. H4. Deep violet blue flowers in May.

St Tudy—(*augustinii* × *impeditum*), AM 1960. H4. The same cross as the last, and to me, virtually indistinguishable from it. Possibly this one is taller, it can reach 7 or 8ft. Both are beautiful plants with intensely coloured, almost luminous flowers; rather like larger Blue Diamonds.

Seta—(*spinuliferum* × *moupinense*), AM 1933, FCC 1960. H4. Unusual, striped pink and white tubular flowers in March and April. Hardy and free-flowering.

Spinulosum—(*spinuliferum* × *racemosum*), AM 1944. H4. Tubular pink flowers with protruding anthers, in April.

Tally Ho—(*eriogynum* × *griersonianum*), FCC 1933. H3. Brilliant red flowers, leaves with a brown indumentum below, silvery new growth. Flowers in June and July, but unfortunately not for cold gardens.

Telstar—(*yakusimanum* × Pauline), AM 1966. Pink and white flowers with a red throat, in May. A compact grower, up to about 4ft.

Temple Belle—(*orbiculare* × *williamsianum*). H3. A neat grower, with rose pink flowers in April and May. Not as hardy as some of the *R. williamsianum* hybrids.

Tensing—(Fabia × Romany Chai), AM 1953. H3. Deep pink flowers with an orange throat in June and July.

Tessa—(Praecox × *moupinense*), AM 1935, AGM 1968. H4. Light and open—growing to 3 or 4ft; flowers larger and deeper pink than those of *Praecox*, in March and April. Tessa Roza (AM 1953) is slightly taller.

Thomwilliams—(*thomsonii* × *williamsianum*). Smallish, with deep pink flowers in April and May, and the rounded foliage that might be expected from its parentage.

Yellowhammer

Vanguard—(*griersonianum* × *venator*). H3. Large brilliant red flowers and dark green foliage. May.

Vesuvius—(*griersonianum* × Romany Chai). Clear, geranium red flowers; more compact than *R. griersonianum*, and hardier than Tally Ho. June and July.

Winsome—(Humming Bird × *griersonianum*), AM 1950. H3–4. Bell-shaped pink flowers opening from red buds, in May. Bronze new growth.

Yellow Hammer—(*flavidum* × *sulfureum*). H4. Can grow to 5 or 6ft, but is columnar rather than spreading. It has bright yellow, narrow, tubular flowers in April.

DWARF HYBRIDS

Blue Bird—(*augustinii* × *intricatum*), AM 1943, AGM 1968. H4. Grows to 3 or 4ft, with a spreading habit. Pale violet blue flowers in April and May.

Blue Pool—(Sapphire × *augustinii*). Lavender blue flowers in April and May; dense and compact.

Blue Star—(*impeditum* × St Tudy). Bright, violet blue flowers in April.

Blue Tit—(*augustinii* × *impeditum*). H4. One of the most easily obtainable of the 'blue' hybrids, but not, I think, one of the best, as the flowers are rather wishy-washy and fade to a slaty colour. Perhaps there are better forms than the ones I have seen.

Bric-a-brac—(*leucaspis* × *moupinense*), AM 1945. H3. A very pretty, early hybrid with milky-white flowers with chocolate anthers; some forms are pale pink. February/March.

Carmen—(*sanguineum* subsp. *didymum* × *forrestii* var. *repens*). H4. Low, spreading and free-flowering, with very dark red, tubular-campanulate flowers in April and May.

Chikor—(*chryseum* × *ludlowii*), AM 1962, FCC 1968. H4. This won the Cory cup in 1962 for the best hybrid of any genus. It grows to about 1ft, and is very free, with primrose yellow flowers in April and May.

Chink—(*keiskei* × *trichocladum*), AM 1961. H4. Greenish-yellow flowers in March and April, and bronze new growth. Reaches about 3ft.

Cilpinense—(*ciliatum* × *moupinense*), AM 1927, FCC 1968. H4. Very much intermediate between the parents, with glossy dark leaves, a neat habit and pink scented flowers in March and April.

Ethel—(F. C. Puddle × *forrestii* var. *repens*), FCC 1940. H3. Prostrate, with scarlet flowers in April, larger than those of *R. forrestii*.

Elisabeth Hobbie—(Essex Scarlet × *forrestii* var. *repens*). H4. Bred in Germany, and extremely hardy, even half-open buds can stand some frost. Bright red flowers in May; grows to about 3ft.

Fittra—(*dauricum* × *racemosum*), AM 1949. H4. Deep pink flowers in April and May; very free-flowering; grows to about 3ft.

Golden Fleece—(*keiskei* × *hanceanum*). Grows only to about 1ft; yellow flowers in April and May.

Impeanum—(*hanceanum* × *impeditum*), FCC 1934. H4. Deep, violet-blue flowers in May.

Intrifast—(*fastigiatum* × *intricatum*). H4. Blue-purple flowers in April.

Lava Flow—(*?sanguineum* subsp. *didymum* × *griersonianum*). Small and compact, with trusses of up to 10 scarlet flowers in July.

Little Ben—(*forrestii* var. *repens* × *neriiflorum*), FCC 1937. H4. Waxy scarlet flowers, freely borne, in April.

Little Bert—(*forestii* var. *repens* × *neriiflorum* var. *euchaites*), AM 1939. H4. A splendid plant, in spite of its unfortunate name. Prostrate, smothered in waxy, scarlet flowers in April.

Martine—(*racemosum* × ? Hinomayo). Clear pink flowers in May. Bred in Holland, so should be ultra-hardy.

Mayfair—(Blue Tit × *impeditum*). H4. Another typical Lapponicum series cross. Lavender-blue flowers in April and May.

Moonstone—(*campylocarpum* × *williamsianum*). H3. Pale yellow bells, flushed with pink in April and May.

Moorheim's Scarlet—(Earl of Athlone × *forrestii* var. *repens*). H4. Prostrate in habit, scarlet bell-shaped flowers in rather sparse trusses. Not as good as Jenny, but presumably ultra-hardy, as it was bred in Germany.

Phalarope—(*pemakoense* × *davidsonianum*), PC 1968. Pale pink flowers that last well on the plant, free-flowering. Grows to about 3ft. April/May.

Pink Drift—(*calostratum* × *scintillans*). H4. Similar to *R. scintillans* in habit, but smothered in pink flowers in May.

Pipit—(*lowndesii* × *lepidotum*). Pink flowers in June; only grows about 6in high.

Prostigiatum—(*prostratum* × *fastigiatum*), AM 1924. H4. Prostrate, with mauve-purple flowers in May. Very free-flowering.

Ptarmigan—(*microleucum* × *leucaspis*), FCC 1965. H4. A very attractive, free-flowering dwarf growing to about 1ft, with white flowers with dark anthers in April.

Racil—(*racemosum* × *ciliatum*). AM 1957. H4. Free-flowering, with blush pink flowers in April.

Rosy Bell—(*ciliatum* × *glaucophyllum*), AM 1894. H4. Another old hybrid with a 'modern' look, like Praecox. Dark, glossy foliage and pink, tubular-campanulate flowers, pleasant rather than showy. Just comes into the 'dwarf' class, as it grows to about 3ft.

Sapphire—(Blue Tit × *impeditum*), AM 1967. H4. Grows to

Rosy Bell

about 2ft; has light blue freely-borne flowers in April
and May.

Sarled—(*sargentianum* × *trichostomum* var. *ledoides*). H4.
Clusters of white flowers opening from pink buds, in
May.

Scarlet Wonder—(*forrestii* var. *repens* × *williamsianum*). H4.
Very low-growing, with rich red flowers. May.

Snow Lady—(*leucaspis* × *ciliatum*). White flowers in March and
April. Grows to about 3ft.

Songbird—(Blue Tit × *russatum*), AM 1957. H4. Has deep,
blue-purple flowers in April and May; grows to about
3ft. 'Songster' is another clone of the same parentage
with paler flowers.

TENDER HYBRIDS, FOR THE
COOL GREENHOUSE

All of these have large flowers, mostly white or pale pink;
many are scented, and many are straggling growers.

Actress—(*bullatum* × Lady Alice Fitzwilliam). The flowers are white inside, stained with red outside, scented. April/ May.

Countess of Haddington—(*ciliatum* × *dalhousiae*), FCC 1862. Fairly small growing; scented pink flowers in April.

Forsterianum—(*edgeworthii* × *veitchianum*). Frilly white flowers with a yellow eye, sweetly scented. Again, fairly small growing. May.

Fragrantissimum—(*edgeworthii* × *formosum*), FCC 1868. H1. Heavily scented white flowers opening from pink buds in May. Fairly small.

Grierdal (*R. griersonianum* × *R. dalhousiae*) is rather a curiosity, as it is one of the very few hybrids between an elepidote and a lepidote species, but it is also an attractive cool house plant, with lax trusses of long-tubed flowers that are an unusual colour; a sort of light vermilion.

Johnnie Johnston—(*johnstoneanum* double form × *tephropeplum*), AM 1946. Pink flowers in May, slightly double.

Lady Alice Fitzwilliam—FCC 1851. H1. Relatively compact. Dark green foliage, pale pink scented flowers with darker stripes. May.

Princess Alice—(*ciliatum* × *edgeworthii*), FCC 1862. White flowers with a yellow eye, tinged with pink in bud, scented. April. Heat tolerant; in parts of the world where it can be grown outside, does better in part shade.

Tyermannii—(*formosum* × *nuttallii*), FCC 1925. A strong grower, with large dark leaves and reddish-brown bark. Large, lily-like white flowers, yellow-throated and heavily scented, in June.

White Wings—(*bullatum* × *ciliicalyx*), AM 1939. The leaves are like those of *R. bullatum*. The flowers are heavily scented, with a yellow eye, in May.

'Grierdal' (*R. griersonianum* × *R. dalhousiae*) is rather a curiosity, as it is one of the few hybrids between an elepidote and a lepidote species. It is a cool house plant, with light vermilion flowers.

Azaleodendrons

The name clings, although they are simply the result of crossing two elepidote series. Most are old hybrids, not grown much now, but still commercially available, and many have beautiful, scented flowers.

Broughtonii aureum—(*maximum* × *ponticum* × *molle*), FCC 1935. Yellow flowers in June.

Dr Masters—(*japonicum* × Prince Camille de Rohan). Salmon, tinged with yellow. June.

Dot. Salmon. June.

Fragrans—(*catawbiense* × *viscosum*). Lilac flowers, sweetly scented, in July.

Galloper Light, AM 1927. Pink flowers in May, fading to yellow.

Glory of Littleworth, AM 1911. Good blue-green foliage; cream flowers spotted with orange, in June.

Govenianum. Deep mauve flowers, scented. July.

Nellie. White flowers in July, with a yellow eye.

Norbitonense aureum. Yellow flowers in June.

HYBRID AZALEAS

Here, again, the choice is so great that only a small number of plants on the market can be mentioned. Many of the varieties are very similar; almost all are worth growing. I have selected some plants from each group that should be fairly easily obtainable, and just give their colour, as more general descriptions of the group are given in the chapter on hybrid azaleas.

Ghent Hybrids

Adolphe—pale pink, orange flare.

Altaclarensis—deep yellow from orange buds, very good autumn colour. Sometimes classed as a Mollis hybrid.

Amabilis—pink and cream, yellow flare.

Bouquet de Flore—salmon pink, white stripe on each petal.

Cardinal—salmon pink, orange flare.

Coccinea speciosa—AGM 1969—vivid orange red, very good.

Corneille—AGM 1969—double pale pink flowers from deeper buds; very good autumn colour.

Crimson King—bright red with orange flare.

Decorator—lilac flushed pink, orange flare.

Electa—salmon orange, yellow flare.

Emma—bright salmon pink, orange flare.

Fanny—magenta pink flowers with red tube and yellow flare; more attractive than that sounds.

Favourite—pinkish orange.

Gloria Mundi—an old variety, bright orange with yellow flare; apt to fade in sun.

Ignea Nova—crimson, with yellow flare.

Nancy Waterer—golden yellow with orange flare; larger flowers than most Ghents.

Narcissiflora—AGM 1969—an old double variety with great charm, pale yellow flowers.

Pallas—orange red.

Prince Henri de Pays Bas—large salmon flowers flushed with red, orange flare. Very late.

Sang de Gentbrugge—bright red.

Splendens—salmon with yellow flare.

Sully—bright rose, yellow flare; very late.

Unique—AM 1952—round trusses of yellow flowers flushed orange, from reddish buds. Very late.

Mollis Azaleas

Adriaan Koster—AM 1935—large yellow flowers, spotted orange.

Alma Tadema—orange, turning pink with age.

Baneuff—salmon with orange flare.

Christopher Wren (Goldball) Yellow, flushed vermilion, from orange-red buds.

Comte de Gomer—(FCC 1879)—pink with orange flare.

Dr M. Oosthoek—AM 1920, AGM 1969. Deep orange red.

Esmeralda—red buds, opening orange.

Floradora—AM 1910—orange-red, darker spots.

Frans van der Bom—orange, opening paler, flushed pink.

J. C. van Tol—bright red.

J. J. de Vinck—AM 1898—red buds opening to golden yellow flowers, spotted red.

Koster's Brilliant Red—self explanatory.

Lemonora—Apricot yellow, flushed red on outside.

Mrs A. E. Endtz—AM 1900—deep yellow, flushed orange, from orange buds.

Mrs Peter Koster—AM 1953—orange red flowers from red buds.

Multatuli—orange red, darker spots.

Princess Juliana—creamy-pink, edged darker pink.

Salmon Queen—salmon pink with orange flare.

Snowdrift—white with orange flare.

Spek's Brilliant—bright orange red.

Spek's Orange—AM 1948, FCC 1953, AGM 1969—orange.

Knaphill and Exbury Azaleas

Albacore—white

Annabella—yellow, flushed orange.

Aurora—pale yellow, flushed pink.

Avon—AM 1958—pale yellow, deeper flare.

Ballerina—pink buds opening to large white flowers with an orange flare.

Balzac—AM 1934—vermilion red with an orange flash; scented.

Basilisk—AM 1934—cream with orange flare.

Beaulieu—deep pink buds, opening paler, orange flare.

Berryrose—AM 1934—pink with a yellow flare.

Brazil—orange red, frilly edged.

Bullfinch—deep rosy red.

Buzzard—yellow, flushed with pink.

Cam—AM 1959—smallish pink semidouble flowers with an orange flare, in a tight round truss.

Cecile—pink with a yellow flare.

Devon—AM 1952—orange red.

Dracula—dark red, from even darker buds.

Eisenhower—vermilion red, orange blotch.

Firefly—deep crimson pink, orange flare.

Fireglow—vermilion orange.

Flarepath—deep red.

Frome—AM 1958—yellow, with red in the throat.

Gallipoli—red buds opening tangerine; orange flare.

Gannet—pink, darker at edges, with orange flare.

George Reynolds—very large yellow flowers with darker spots, from pinkish buds. A parent of many of the Exbury hybrids.

Gibraltar—orange red.

Ginger—orange from red buds.

Goldeneye—rich yellow, from orange-red buds.

Golden Horn—pale yellow, flushed pink.

Golden Oriole—AM 1947—deep gold, orange flare.

Homebush—AM 1950, AGM 1969—deep pink, double flowers.

Hotspur—AM 1934—large, rich orange-red flowers.

Hugh Wormald—bright yellow with orange flare.

J. Jennings—deep orange-vermilion flowers.

Kathleen—large, salmon pink flowers with orange flare.

Kestrel—orange red.

Klondyke—orange, flushed red.

Knighthood—AM 1943—rich orange red.

Lady Derby—cream fading to white; orange blotch.

Lady Rosebery—brilliant crimson.

Lapwing—creamy yellow, flushed pink.

Marion Merriman—AM 1925—yellow with an orange flare.

Medway—AM 1959—pale pink, frilly, deeper at edges; orange flare.

Nancy Buchanan—creamy white, yellow flare.

Old Gold—yellow flushed red, orange flare.

Orange Truffles—apricot flushed vermilion outside, double.

Oxydol—white, yellow spots.

Penguin—yellow flushed pink.

Persil—white, orange flare.

Redshank—orange red, yellow blotch.

Royal Lodge—vermilion, darkening with age.

Ruddy Duck—salmon pink; bronze young foliage.

Rumba—orange.

Silver Slipper—AM 1962, FCC 1963—white flushed pink, orange flare.

Stour—AM 1958—orange red, frilly.

Strawberry Ice—AM 1963, AGM 1969—pink, deeper edged, yellow flare.

Tay—very large, rich yellow, frilly flowers in round trusses.

Thames—AM 1958—large flat pink flowers, with orange flare.

Trent—AM 1958—yellow, edged salmon.

Whitethroat—AM 1962—double white.

Wryneck—yellow, tinged pink.

The varieties with names of rivers have been bred at Wisley; those with names of birds at Knaphill nursery.

Occidentale Hybrids

Delicatissima—large trusses of cream flowers, flushed pink, with an orange flare.

Exquisita—AM 1950, FCC 1968. Large trusses of pale pink flowers, darker on the outside; orange flare.

Graciosa—AM 1905—creamy yellow, flushed pink, from deep pink buds.

Irene Koster—pale pink, long-tubed flowers, flushed with deeper pink and yellow.

Magnifica—creamy white, flushed pink, orange flare.

Rosea—long-tubed white flowers, marked with pink.

Superba—large trusses of frilly pink flowers with an apricot blotch.

Rustica Flore Pleno

Aida—deep pink with a lilac tinge.

Byron—AM 1953—white, flushed pink.

Freya—AM 1897 & 1953—pale pink, tinged salmon.

Il Tasso—rose, tinged salmon.

Norma—AM 1891 & 1959, AGM 1969. Bright rose pink, from red buds.

Phoebe—pale yellow, from deeper buds.

Phidias—cream flushed pink, from pink buds.

Ribera—AM 1917 & 1953—rose pink flowers with a yellow throat, paling with age.

Evergreen Azaleas

There seem to be even more hybrids of these than there are of deciduous azaleas; again, only a small selection is practicable. Hardiness ratings are given where known.

Kurume Azaleas

THE WILSON FIFTY

1 Seikai (Madonna), H4, white, hose-in-hose.
2 Kure-no-yuki (Snowflake), H4, AGM 1969, AM 1952. White, hose-in-hose.
3 Shin Seikai (Old Ivory), H4, AM 1921 & 1952. Cream.
4 Yorozuyo (Purity)—greenish white.
5 Nani Wagata (Painted Lady)—mauve.
6 Tancho.
7 Hachika Tsugi (Prudence)—lilac with white throat.
8 Irohayama (Dainty)—H4, AM 1952, rosy-lavender, faint chestnut eye.
9 Hoo (Apple Blossom)—H3, AM 1952, pink with white throat.
10 Suiyohi (Sprite)—H3, pink, red spots, white anthers.
11 Takasago (Cherry Blossom)—H4, lilac, deeper edge.
12 Kasume Gaseki (Elf)—shell pink.
13 Bijinsui (Little Imp)—H3, pink, brown spotting.
14 Asagasumi—H3, crimson-pink, hose-in-hose.
15 Kimigayo (Cherub)—H4, mauve-pink, marked red.
16 Azuma Kagami (Pink Pearl)—H3, 1950, AGM 1969.

Salmon pink, chestnut spots, hose-in-hose. Taller than most—to about 5ft.

17 Osaraku (Penelope)—rose-lavender, darker centre.

18 Otome (Maiden's Blush)—lilac-pink.

19 Aya Kammuri (Pinkie)—H4, salmon, white anthers.

20 Shintoki-no-hagasane (Rose Taffeta)—pink, deeper centre, red stamens.

21 Saotome (Peach Blossom)—H4, rose-lavender.

22 Kirin (Coral Bells or Daybreak)—H3, AM 1952, AGM 1968. Rose pink, red anthers, hose-in-hose.

23 Tamafuyo (Fancy)—white, brown stamens.

24 Kiritsubo (Twilight)—H4, rose-lavender.

25 Omoine (Dame Lavender)—lilac, white throat.

26 Oino Mezame (Melody)—bright mauve pink.

27 Katsura-no-hana (Ruth)—lilac pink, white anthers.

28 Shin Utena (Santo)—H4, AM 1952, lilac, deeper edged.

29 Komo-no-uye (Salmon Prince)—H4, salmon pink.

30 Beinfude.

31 Suga-no-ito (Betty)—H4, AM 1952, pale lilac, chestnut eye.

32 Kasane Kagaribi (Rosita)—deep rose pink.

33 Tsuta Momiji (Cardinal)—rose pink, hose-in-hose.

34 Suetsumu (Flame)—bright salmon red.

35 Fudesute-yama—H4, light red.

36 Ima Shojo (Christmas Cheer)—H4, crimson.

37 Rashomon (Meteor)—H4, large, salmon red flowers, dark anthers.

38 Waka-kayede (Red Robin)—H4, magenta.

39 Yayehioya.

40 Kurai-no-himo (Carmine Queen)—H3, large, crimson flowers, hose-in-hose.

41 Agemaki (Jose)—crimson.

42 Hinodegiri (Red Hussar)—H4, AM 1965, AGM 1969. Brilliant red.

43 Aioi (Fairy Queen)—lavender pink, hose-in-hose.

44 Sakura Tsukasa (Allglow)—large lavender flowers, pale anthers.

45 Tama-no-utena (Flamingo)—salmon pink, crimson spots.

46 Gosho Zakura (Vanity)—deep pink flowers, darker spots.

47 Ukamuse (Princess Delight)—H4, AM 1952. Salmon, white eye.

48 Hinode-no-taka (Ruby)—H4. Magenta pink, white anthers.

49 Osaraku seedling (Winsome)—Pale lavender, deeper edges.

50 Hana-asobi—H4, rose red, white anthers.

Other Kurume Varieties

Azafujin—H4; pink, flushed deeper pink.

Benigiri—H4; crimson.

Bikini—H4; peach pink.

Colyer—H4; AM 1959, magenta purple.

Esmeralda—H4; pale pink, hose-in-hose.

Fude Tsuka—H4; pink, cream throat, hose-in-hose.

Fukohiko—H4; crimson.

Harumo-kyoki—H4; low and spreading, white.

Hatsugiri—H4; AM 1956, FCC 1969, magenta purple; dwarf.

Hino Crimson—H4; crimson.

Hinomayo—H4; AM 1921, FCC 1945, AGM 1954. Large pink flowers, very profuse. Can grow to 4 or 5ft.

Izumigawa—H4; lilac with red spots, paler in throat.

Kirishima—H4; pink or mauve.

Kure-no-yuki—H4; AM 1952, AGM 1968. White, hose-in-hose.

Lady Elphinstone—H4; AM 1952. Crimson-pink.

Miyagino—H4; deep pink, hose-in-hose; low and spreading.

Port Knap—H4; AM 1958. Purple.

Vida Brown—H4; AM 1962. Rose red.

Kaempferi Hybrids

Addy Wery—H4; AM 1950; bright red.

Alice—H4; salmon red, dark flare.

Anny—H4; AM 1948; orange red.

Arendsii—H4; purple.

Atalanta—H4; lilac.

Bengal Fire—H3; fiery red. *(kaempferi* × *oldhamii)*

Betty—H4; AM 1940; pinkish orange, darker eye.

Betty Loo—H3; pale pink.

Blaauw's Pink—H4; large salmon pink flowers, hose-in-hose.

Blue Danube—H4; bluish purple.

Carmen—H4; pink, darker throat.

Charlotte—H4; deep orange-red.

Cleopatra—H4; bright pink.

Eddie—H3; AM 1944; red, tall growing, tends to fade in sun.

Favorite—H4; deep pink.

Fedora—H4; AM 1931, FCC 1960. Large, bright pink flowers.

Fidelio—H4; deep pink.

Frieda—H4; reddish purple.

Garden Beauty—H4; soft pink.

Gretchen—H4; deep mauve.

Henrietta—H4; rose pink.

Ivette—H4; pink.

Jeanette—H4; AM 1948; large pink flowers, spotted red.

John Cairns—H4; AM 1940, AGM 1952. Brick red—a very distinctive colour—tall growing.

Kathleen—H4; AM 1962, AGM 1968. Rose red.

Leo—H4; salmon orange, dwarf and spreading, late.

Louise—H4; salmon red.

May King—H4; crimson.

May Queen—H4; pink.

Mikado—H4 ; orange-salmon, late.

Mimi—H4 ; pink.

Naomi—H4 ; salmon pink, late.

Nelly—H4 ; light orange.

Nora—H4 ; orange red.

Oberon—H4 ; soft pink.

Ophelia—H4 ; salmon.

Orange Beauty—H4 ; AM 1945, AGM 1968; orange (*kaempferi* × Hinodegiri).

Orange Favourite—H4 ; pink, flushed orange.

Orange King—H4 ; reddish orange.

Pink Treasure—H4 ; pink.

Polar Haven—H4 ; white.

Red Pimpernel—H4 ; red.

Sakata Red—H4 ; AM 1952 ; red. (*kaempferi* × a kurume)

Sakata Rose—H4 ; rose pink. (*kaempferi* × a kurume)

Sir William Lawrence—H4 ; AM 1958; cerise, tall growing; (*kaempferi* × a kurume)

Spring Beauty—H4 ; pink, flushed red.

Surprise—H4 ; orange red.

White Lady—H4 ; white.

Willy—H4 ; soft pink.

Yachiyo—H4 ; lavender, hose-in-hose.

Zampa—H4 ; orange red.

Satsuki and Wada Hybrids

Bungo-mishiki—H4 ; brick red, late.

Chichibu—H4 ; white, hose-in-hose.

Heiwa—H4 ; purple, hose-in-hose.

Kusudama—H4 ; magenta, white throat.

Pink Delight—H3 ; pink.

Shinnyo-no-hikari—H4 ; large white flowers with purple spots.

Tatsumi-no-hikari—H4 ; large white, pink spots.

Indicum Hybrids

Akatasuki—large pink flowers, late June.

Asagi—large, deep rose.

Balsaminiflorum—H3; salmon red, double. A form of *R. indicum* rather than a hybrid. Leaves have long white hairs.

Hamachidori—large, crimson pink flowers.

Hexe (Firefly)—AM 1907; crimson, hose-in-hose; fairly tall.

Isochidari—pink edged white, spotted red.

Kokin-shita—H4; orange. Possibly also a form of *R. indicum.*

Mother's Day—H4; double red. AM 1959, AGM 1968. (*R. indicum* × a kurume)

Purple Queen—deep purple, hose-in-hose.

Glenn Dale Hybrids

Ambrosia—pink, paling to apricot.

Arcadia—H3; deep pink, small flowered.

Buccaneer—H3; orange red, darker flare.

Challenger—orange red, flushed mauve.

Chanticleer—purple.

Content—H3; pink, white eye.

Darkness—brick red, crimson blotch; compact.

Dauntless—purple, scarlet eye; compact.

Elizabeth—pink, spreading.

Harbinger—rose.

Louise Dowdle—bright pink, darker blotch.

Martha Hitchcock—H3; white, lilac edge, late.

Merlin—magenta pink.

Polar Sea—white, frilly, green blotch.

Sagittarius—H3; pink, flushed salmon.

Scout—H3; pale pink.

Tanager—bright red, dark flare.

Gable Hybrids

Herbert—H4; reddish purple, hose-in-hose.

Isabel—H3; double pink.

James Gable—H3; red, dark blotch, hose-in-hose.

Lorna—H3; double pink.

Louise Gable—double salmon pink.

Rosebud—H3; double pale pink.

Stewartianum—H3; clear red.

Vuyk Hybrids

Beethoven—H4; magenta.

Double Beauty—H3; double pink, large-flowered.

Johann Sebastian Bach—H3; purple.

Johann Strauss—H4; deep pink.

Mozart—H4; rose pink.

Palestrina—H4; AM 1944, FCC 1967, AGM 1968. Large white flowers with a green eye, bright green leaves, a lovely plant.

Prince Bernhard—H4; flame red.

Princess Beatrix—H3; orange.

Princess Irene—H4; geranium red.

Princess Juliana—H4; orange red.

Purple Splendour—H4; magenta purple, hose-in-hose.

Purple Triumph—H4; AM 1960; deep purple.

Queen Wilhelmina—H4; deep vermilion, dwarf.

Schubert—H4; bright pink.

Sibelius—H4; orange red.

Vuyk's Rosy Red—H4; AM 1962; rosy red.

Vuyk's Scarlet—H4; AM 1959, FCC 1966, AGM 1968; scarlet.

Other Types

Crispiflorum—crimson pink, hose-in-hose. Probably a form of *R. simsii*.

Gumpo—H3 ; AM 1934 ; white.

Gumpo Red—H3 ; pink !

Fancy Gumpo—H3 ; frilly, pale pink flowers, marked with deeper pink. The Gumpo varieties are possibly forms of *R. simsii*.

Yugiri—H3 ; (*R. simsii* ×) ; pink.

It is unfortunate that there has been some duplication of names in hybrid azaleas, for example, Esmeralda is the name both of a kurume and a mollis hybrid and Betty of a kurume and a kaempferi hybrid. Lady Rosebery is shared by a Knaphill azalea and a hybrid rhododendron.

Rhododendrons Known to be in Cultivation, in Their Series

(This classification is likely to be altered in the near future)

1 Albiflorum series (e)

2 Anthopogon series (l)
   anthopogon
   cephalanthum
   collettianum
   hypenanthum
   kongboense
   laudandum
   primuliflorum
   sargentianum
   trichostomum

3 Arboreum series (e)
Subseries *arboreum*
   arboreum
   delavayi
   lanigerum

   niveum
   peramoenum
   wattii
   zeylanicum
Subseries *argyrophyllum*
   argyrophyllum
   coryanum
   farinosum
   floribundum
   hunnewellianum
   hypoglaucum
   insigne
   rirei
   simiarum
   thayerianum

4 Auriculatum series (e)
   auriculatum

5 Azalea series (e)
Subseries *canadense*
  albrechtii
  canadense
  pentaphyllum
  vaseyi
Subseries *luteum*
  alabamense
  arborescens
  atlanticum
  austrinum
  bakeri
  calendulaceum
  canescens
  luteum
  molle
  nudiflorum
  oblongifolium
  occidentale
  prunifolium
  roseum
  serrulatum
  speciosum
  viscosum
Subseries *nipponicum*
  nipponicum
Subseries *obtusum*
  indicum
  kaempferi
  kiusianum
  linearifolium
  microphyton
  nakaharai
  obtusum
  oldhamii
  pulchrum
  rubropilosum
  scabrum
  serpyllifolium
  simsii

  tosaense
  tschonoskii
  yedoense
Subseries *schlippenbachii*
  amagianum
  dilatatum
  farrerae
  mariesii
  nudipes
  quinquefolium
  reticulatum
  sanctum
  schlippenbachii
  wadanum
  weyrichii
Subseries *tashiroi*

6 Barbatum series (e)
Subseries *barbatum*
  argipeplum
  barbatum
  imberbe
  smithii
Subseries *crinigerum*
  bainbridgeanum
  crinigerum
Subseries *glischrum*
  diphrocalyx
  erosum
  exasperatum
  glischroides
  glischrum
  habrotrichum
  hirtipes
  rude
  spilotum
  vesiculiferum
Subseries *maculiferum*
  anwheiense
  longesquamatum

maculiferum
monosematum
morii
nankotaisanense
pachytrichum
pseudochrysanthum
strigillosum

7 Boothii series (l)
Subseries *boothii*
boothii
chrysodoron
mishmiense
sulfureum
Subseries *megeratum*
leucaspis
megeratum
auritum
chrysolepis
tephropeplum
xanthostephanum

8 Camelliaeflorum series (l)
camelliaeflorum

9 Campanulatum series (e)
campanulatum
fulgens
lanatum
sheriffii
succothii
tsariense
wallichii

10 Campylogynum series (l)
campylogynum

11 Camtschaticum series (e)
camtschaticum

12 Carolinianum series (l)
carolinianum
chapmanii
minus

13 Cinnabarinum series (l)
cinnabarinum
concatens
keysii
xanthocodon

14 Dauricum series (l)
dauricum
mucronulatum

15 Edgeworthii series (l)
bullatum
edgeworthii
pendulum
seinghkuense

16 Falconeri series (e)
arizelum
basilicum
coriaceum
decipiens
eximium
falconeri
fictolacteum
galactinum
hodgsonii
preptum
rex

17 Ferrugineum series (l)
ferrugineum
hirsutum
kotschyi

18 Fortunei series (e)
Subseries *calophytum*
calophytum
Subseries *davidii*
davidii
planetum
praevernum
sutchuense

Subseries *fortunei*
  chlorops
  decorum
  diaprepes
  discolor
  fortunei
  hemsleyanum
  houlstonii
  serotinum
  vernicosum
Subseries *griffithianum*
  griffithianum
Subseries *orbiculare*
  cardiobasis
  orbiculare
Subseries *oreodoxa*
  erubescens
  fargesii
  oreodoxa
  praeteritum

19 Fulvum series (e)
  fulvum
  uvariifolium

20 Glaucophyllum series (l)
Subseries *genestierianum*
  genestierianum
  micromeres
Subseries *glaucophyllum*
  brachyanthum
  charitopes
  glaucophyllum
  shweliense
  tsangpoense

21 Grande series (e)
  coryphaeum
  giganteum
  grande
  macabeanum
  magnificum
  mollyanum
  peregrinum
  praestans
  protistum
  pudorosum
  semnoides
  sidereum
  sinogrande
  watsonii

22 Griersonianum series (e)
  griersonianum

23 Heliolepis series (l)
  bracteatum
  brevistylum
  desquamatum
  fumidum
  heliolepis
  oporinum
  pholidotum
  rubiginosum

24 Irroratum series (e)
Subseries *irroratum*
  aberconwayi
  agastum
  annae
  anthosphaerum
  araiophyllum
  dimitrum
  eritimum
  hardingii
  irroratum
  kendrickii
  laxiflorum
  lukiangense
  ningyuenense
  pankimense
  pennivenium

pogonostylum
ramsdenianum
shepherdii
tanastylum
Subseries *parishii*
   agapetum
   cookeianum
   elliottii
   eriogynum
   facetum
   kyawi
   parishii
   schistocalyx
   venator

25 Lacteum series (e)
   agglutinatum
   beesianum
   dictyotum
   dryophyllum
   dumulosum
   lacteum
   phaeochrysum
   przewalskii
   traillianum
   wightii

26 Lappnicum series (l)
   achroanthum
   alpicola
   blepharocalyx
   capitatum
   chamaezelum
   chryseum
   compactum
   complexum
   cuneatum
   dasypetalum
   diacritum
   drumonium
   edgarianum

fastigiatum
fimbriatum
flavidum
glomerulatum
hippophaeoides
idoneum
impeditum
intricatum
lapponicum
litangense
lysolepis
microleucum
nigropunctatum
nitidulum
nivale
oresbium
orthocladum
paludosum
parvifolium
peramabile
polifolium
ramosissimum
ravum
rupicola
russatum
scintillans
setosum
spilanthum
stictophyllum
tapetiforme
telmateium
thymifolium
verruculosum
violaceum
websterianum
yungingense

27 Lepidotum series (l)
Subseries *baileyi*
   baileyi

Subseries *lepidotum*
  lepidotum
  lowndesii

28 Maddenii series (l)
Subseries *ciliicalyx*
  burmanicum
  carneum
  ciliatum
  ciliicalyx
  cubittii
  cuffeanum
  dendricola
  fletcherianum
  formosum
  inaequale
  iteophyllum
  johnstoneanum
  lasiopodum
  lyi
  pachypodum
  parryae
  scopulorum
  scottianum
  supranubium
  surasianum
  taronense
  valentinianum
  veitchianum
Subseries *maddenii*
  brachysiphon
  crassum
  maddenii
  manipurense
  odoriferum
  polyandrum
Subseries *megacalyx*
  dalhousiae
  headfortianum
  lindleyi

megacalyx
nuttallii
rhabdotum
sinonuttallii
taggianum

29 Micranthum series (l)
  micranthum

30 Moupinense series (l)
  moupinense

31 Neriiflorum series (e)
Subseries *forrestii*
  chamae-thomsonii
  forrestii
Subseries *haematodes*
  beanianum
  catacosum
  chaetomallum
  chionanthum
  coelicum
  haematodes
  hemidartum
  mallotum
  pocophorum
Subseries *neriiflorum*
  albertsenianum
  floccigerum
  neriiflorum
  sperabile
  sperabiloides
Subseries *sanguineum*
  aperantum
  citriniflorum
  dichroanthum
  eudoxum
  fulvastrum
  parmulatum
  sanguineum
  temenium

32 Ovatum series (e)
   leptothrium
   ovatum

33 Ponticum series (e)
Subseries *caucasicum*
   adenopodum
   brachycarpum
   caucasicum
   chrysanthum
   degronianum
   fauriei
   hyperythrum
   makinoi
   metternichii
   smirnowi
   ungernii
   yakusimanum
Subseries *ponticum*
   catawbiense
   macrophyllum
   maximum
   ponticum

34 Saluense series (l)
   calostratum
   chameunum
   fragariflorum
   keleticum
   nitens
   prostratum
   radicans
   saluense

35 Scabrifolium series (l)
   hemitrichotum
   mollicomum
   pubescens
   racemosum
   scabrifolium

   spiciferum
   spinuliferum

36 Semibarbatum series (e)
   semibarbatum

37 Stamineum series
   championae
   moulmainense
   oxyphyllum
   pectinatum
   stamineum
   stenaulum
   wilsonae

38 Taliense series (e)
Subseries *adenogynum*
   adenogynum
   adenophorum
   alutaceum
   balfourianum
   bureauvii
   bureavioides
   detersile
   detonsum
   faberi
   mimetes
   prattii
   wuense
Subseries *roxieanum*
   bathyphyllum
   globigerum
   gymnocarpum
   iodes
   microgynum
   pronum
   proteoides
   recurvoides
   roxieanum
   russotinctum
   triplonaevium
   tritifolium

Subseries *taliense*
 aganniphum
 clementinae
 doshongense
 flavorufum
 glaucopeplum
 schizopeplum
 sphaeroblastum
 taliense
 vellereum
Subseries *wasonii*
 inopinum
 paradoxum
 rufum
 wasonii
 weldianum
 wiltonii

39 Thomsonii series (e)
Subseries *campylocarpum*
 callimorphum
 caloxanthum
 campylocarpum
 myiagrum
 panteumorphum
 telopeum
Subseries *cerasinum*
 cerasinum
Subseries *selense*
 dasycladum
 erythrocalyx
 esetulosum
 eurysyphon
 jucundum
 martinianum
 selense
 setiferum
 vestitum
Subseries *souliei*
 litiense

 puralbum
 souliei
 wardii
Subseries *thomsonii*
 cyanocarpum
 eclecteum
 hookeri
 hylaeum
 lopsangianum
 meddianum
 stewartianum
 thomsonii
 viscidifolium
Subseries *williamsianum*
 williamsianum

40 Trichocladum series (l)
 caesium
 chloranthum
 cowanianum
 lepidostylum
 lophogynum
 mekongense
 melinanthum
 oulotrichum
 rubrolineatum
 semilunatum
 trichocladum
 viridescens

41 Triflorum series (l)
Subseries *augustinii*
 augustinii
 trichanthum
Subseries *hanceanum*
 hanceanum
Subseries *triflorum*
 ambiguum
 bauhiniiflorum
 flavantherum
 kasoense

keiskei
lutescens
triflorum
Subseries *yunnanense*
   amesiae
   bodinieri
   concinnoides
   concinnum
   davidsonianum
   hormophorum
   hypophaeum
   longistylum
   oreotrephes
   polylepis
   rigidum
   searsiae
   siderophyllum

tatsienense
vilmorinianum
yunnanense
zaleucum

42 Uniflorum series (l)
   imperator
   ludlowii
   patulum
   pemakoense
   pumilum
   uniflorum

43 Vaccinioides series (l)
   vaccinioides

44 Virgatum series (l)
   oleifolium
   virgatum

Classification

The following is a review of the classification of the genus *Rhododendron* according to Sleumer (1949), showing how it relates to the series of Stevenson (1947) and Cowan & Davidian (1947–56). It is taken from the paper by Almut Seithe. After it, is a list of the series and their component species that is in general horticultural use.

This may not interest many readers, but the Sleumer classification is not readily available in English, and so it seemed worth including.

Chorus subgenerum *Rhododendron*
  Subgenus *Rhododendron*
    Section *Rhododendron*
      Subsection *Rhododendron*   (= Series *Ferrugineum* Hutch.)
      Subsection *Boothia* (Hutch.) Sleum.   (= Series *Boothii* Hutch. Subseries *Boothii* and
                                              Megeratum Cowan and David.)
      Subsection *Tephropepla* (Cowan and David.) (= Series *Boothii* Hutch. Subseries *Tephropeplum* Cowan
        Sleum.   and David.)
      Subsection *Camelliaeflora* (Hutch.) Sleum. (= Series *Camelliaeflorum* Hutch.)
      Subsection *Campylogyna* (Hutch.) Sleum. (= Series *Campylogynum* Hutch.)
      Subsection *Caroliniana* (Hutch.) Sleum. (= Series *Carolinianum* Hutch.)
      Subsection *Cinnabarina* (Hutch.) Sleum. (= Series *Cinnabarinum* Hutch.)

Subsection *Edgeworthia* (Hutch.) Sleum. (= Series *Edgeworthii* Hutch.)

Subsection *Glauca* (Hutch.) Sleum. (= Series *Glaucum* Hutch. Subseries *Glaucum* Cowan and David.)

Subsection *Genesteriana* (Cowan and David.) Sleum. (= Series *Glaucum* Hutch. Subseries *Genesterianum* Cowan and David.)

Subsection *Heliolepida* (Hutch.) Sleum. (= Series *Heliolepis* Hutch.)

Subsection *Lapponica* (Hutch.) Sleum. (= Series *Lapponicum* Hutch.)

Subsection *Lepidota* (Hutch.) Sleum. (= Series *Lepidotum* Hutch. Subseries *Lepidotum* Cowan and David.)

Subsection *Baileya* (Cowan and David.) Sleum. (= Series *Lepidotum* Hutch. Subseries *Baileyi* Cowan and David.)

Subsection *Uniflora* (Cowan and David.) Sleum. (= Series *Lepidotum* Hutch. pr. pte. = *Uniflorum* Cowan and David.)

Subsection *Maddenia* (Hutch.) Sleum. (= Series *Maddenii* Hutch.)

Subsection *Micrantha* (Hutch.) Sleum. (= Series *Micranthum* Hutch.)

Subsection *Moupinensia* (Hutch.) Sleum. (= Series *Moupinense* Hutch.)

Subsection *Saluenensia* (Hutch.) Sleum. (= Series *Saluenense* Hutch.)

Subsection *Triflora* (Hutch.) Sleum. (= Series *Triflorum* Hutch.)

Section *Pogonanthum* G. Don (= Series *Anthopogon* Hutch and *Cephalanthum* Hutch. = Series Anthopogon (Hutch.) Cowan and David.)

Section *Vireya* (Blume) H. F. Copeland

Subsection *Vireya* (—)

Subsection *Astrovireya* Sleum. (—)

Subsection *Leiovireya* Copeland (—)

Subsection *Linearanthera* Copeland (= Series *Vaccanioides* Hutch. pr. pte.)

Subsection *Linnaeopsis* (Schlecht.) Sleum. ( )
Subsection *Malayovireya* Sleum. ( )
Subsection *Phaeovireya* Sleum. ( )
Subsection *Pseudovireya* (C. B. Clarke) Sleum. (= Series *Vaccinioides* Hutch. pr. pte.)
Subsection *Schizovireya* Sleum. ( )
Subsection *Solenovireya* Copeland. ( )

Subgenus *Pseudazalea* Sleum. (= Series *Trichocladum* Hutch.)
Subgenus *Rhodorastrum* (Maxim.) C. B. Clarke (= *Dauricum* Hutch.)
Subgenus *Pseudorhodorastrum* Sleum.
 Section *Pseudorhodorastrum* (= Series *Virgatum* Hutch. pr. pte.)
 Section *Rhodobotrys* Sleum. (= Series *Virgatum* Hutch. pr. pte.)
 Section *Trachyrhodion* Sleum. (= Series *Scabrifolium* Hutch.)

Chorus subgenerum Azalea (L.) Seithe-v. Hoff
Subgenus *Azalea*
 Section *Azalea* (= Series *Azalea* Rehd. Subseries *Luteum* Rehd.)
 Section *Rhodora* (L.) G. Don (= Series *Azalea* Rehd. Subseries *Canadense* Rehd.)
 Section *Viscidula* Mats. and Nak. (= Series *Azalea* Rehd. Subseries *Nipponicum* Rehd.)
Subgenus *Tsutsia* Planch.
 Section *Tsutsia* (= Series *Azalea* Rehd. Subseries *Obtusum* Rehd.)
 Section *Brachycalyx* Sweet (= Series *Azalea* Rehd. Subseries *Schlippenbachii* Rehd.)
 Section *Tsusiopsis* Sleum. (= Series *Azalea* Rehd. Subseries *Tashiroi* Rehd.)
Subgenus *Azaleastrum* Planch.
 Section *Azaleastrum* (= Series *Ovatum* Hutch.)
 Section *Choniastrum* Franch. (= Series *Stamineum* Hutch.)
 Section *Candidastrum* Sleum. (= Series *Albiflorum* Rehd.)
 Section *Mumeazalea* (Makino) Sleum. (= Series *Semibarbatum* Rehd.)

Chorus subgenerum *Hymenanthes* (Bl.) Seith-v. Hoff

Subgenus *Hymenanthes*
  Section *Hymenanthes*
    Subsection *Hymenanthes*   (= Series *Ponticum* Tagg)
    Subsection *Arborea* (Tagg) Sleum.   (= Series *Arboreum* Tagg Subseries *Arboreum* Tagg)
    Subsection *Argyrophylla* (Tagg) Sleum.   (= Series *Arboreum* Tagg Subseries *Argyrophyllum* Tagg pr. pte.)

    Subsection *Floribunda* (Tagg) Sleum.   (= Series *Arboreum* Tagg Subseries *Argyrophyllum* Tagg pr. pte.)

    Subsection *Auriculata* (Tagg) Sleum.   (= Series *Auriculatum* Tagg)
    Subsection *Barbata* (Tagg) Sleum.   (= Series *Barbatum* Tagg Subseries *Barbatum, Glischrum* and *Crinigerum* Tagg)

    Subsection *Maculifera* (Tagg) Sleum.   (= Series *Barbatum* Tagg Subseries *Maculiferum* Tagg)
    Subsection *Campanulata* (Tagg) Sleum.   (= Series *Campanulatum* Tagg)
    Subsection *Falconera* (Tagg) Sleum.   (= Series *Falconeri* Tagg)
    Subsection *Fortunea* (Tagg) Sleum.   (= Series *Fortunei* Tagg)
    Subsection *Fulva* (Tagg) Sleum.   (= Series *Fulvum* Tagg)
    Subsection *Grandia* (Tagg) Sleum.   (= Series *Grande* Tagg)
    Subsection *Irrorata* (Tagg) Sleum.   (= Series *Irroratum* Tagg Subseries *Irroratum* Tagg)
    Subsection *Parishia* (Tagg) Sleum.   (= Series *Irroratum* Tagg Subseries *Parishii* Tagg)
    Subsection *Lactea* (Tagg) Sleum.   (= Series *Lacteum* Tagg)
    Subsection *Neriiflora* (Tagg) Sleum.   (= Series *Neriiflorum* Tagg)
    Subsection *Taliensia* (Tagg) Sleum.   (= Series *Taliense* Tagg)
    Subsection *Thomsonia* (Tagg) Sleum.   (= Series *Thomsonii* Tagg Subseries *Thomsonii* Tagg)
    Subsection *Campylocarpa* (Tagg) Sleum. (= Series *Thomsonii* Tagg Subseries *Campylocarpum* Tagg)
    Subsection *Martiniana* (Tagg) Sleum.   (= Series *Thomsonii* Tagg Subseries *Martinianum* Tagg)
    Subsection *Selensia* (Tagg) Sleum.   (= Series *Thomsonii* Tagg Subseries *Selense* Tagg)
    Subsection *Souliea* (Tagg) Sleum.   (= Series *Thomsonii* Tagg Subseries *Souliei* Tagg)

APPENDIX 3

Where to Buy Rhododendrons

BRITAIN

Most nurseries and garden centres have some rhododendrons, hardy hybrids in particular, and often some of the dwarf hybrids, such as Hummingbird. There must be many more nurseries than those I have listed which can supply more than that, but I think the list includes all or most of the real specialists.

E. H. M. & P. A. Cox, Glendoick Garden Ltd, Perth, Scotland

M. Haworth-Booth, Farall Nurseries, Roundhurst, Haslemere, Surrey

Hillier & Sons, Winchester, Hants

Hydon Nurseries Ltd, Hydon Heath, near Godalming, Surrey

W. Th. Ingwerson, Birch Farm Nursery, Gravetye, East Grinstead, Sussex, RH19 4LE
Only dwarf species and hybrids, but a good selection of these.

Paton & King, Barnhourie, Colvend, Dalbeattie, Kirkcudbrightshire
Again, only dwarfs.

Knap Hill Nursery Ltd, Barrs Lane, Knap Hill, Woking, Surrey
Particularly good for deciduous azalea hybrids.

J. R. Ponton, The Gardens, Kirknewton, Midlothian
Like Birch Farm Nursery, basically an alpine nursery with a good selection of dwarf rhododendrons.

G. Reuthe Ltd, Foxhill Nurseries, Keston, Kent, BR2 6AW
As well as a vast selection of species, they stock a lot of the more modern hybrids.

Walter C. Slocock Ltd, Goldsworth Nurseries, Woking, Surrey

Sunningdale Nurseries, Windlesham, Surrey

Waterers, Bagshot, Surrey
Mostly hybrids.

AMERICA

Tumble Brook Rhododendron Nursery, 365 Simsbury Rd, Bloomfield, Conn. 06002

Angelica Nurseries, RFD, 1, Mohnton, Pa.

Joseph B. Gable, Stewartstown, Pa.

G. G. Nearing, Box 402, Ramsey, New Jersey

Azalea Gardens, R. A. West, 92045 29th St, RFD, 1, Scotts, Mich.

Northern Azalea Gardens, 823 DeGroff St, Grand Lodge, Mich.

A. Shammarello & Son Nursery, 4590 Monticello Blvd, South Euclid St, Ohio

Haddock Nursery, Box 603, Silver Spring, Md.

The Bovees, S.W. Coronado St. & 16th Drive, Portland, Oregon

George W. Clarke, 11740 N.E. Marine Drive, Portland, Oregon 97220

Comerford's, Box 100, Marion, Oregon

Henny & Wennekamp Inc, Box 212, Brooks, Oregon

Irving B. Lincoln, 221 American Bank Bldg, Portland 5, Oregon

Gilbert & June Zolling, 6750 S.W. Oleson Rd, Portland, Oregon

Island Gardens, 701 Goodpasture Island Rd, Eugene, Oregon 97401

J. B. Whalley Nursery, R.2, Box 683, Troutdale, Oregon 97060

Bonnybrook Nursery, 14237 100th Ave, N.E. Bothell, Wash.

J. Harold Clarke, Long Beach, Wash.

Flora Markeeta, 22925 102nd Place West, Edmonds, Wash.

Rainier Mt. Alpine Gardens, 2007 S. 126th St, Seattle 88, Wash.

Seven Firs Nursery, RFD, 1, Box 147, North Bend, Wash.

Kammer's, 403–49th Ave N.E., Puyallup, Wash.

John S. Druecker Nurseries, Box 511, Fort Bragg, Calif.

Indian Run Nursery, Robbinsville, N.J. 08691

Redbarn Nursery, 579 Main St, Pennsburg, Pa.

Royer Greenhouses, West St, Doylestown, Pa. 18901

CANADA

Layritz Nurseries Ltd, RR3, Victoria, B.C.

Royston Nursery, Box 228, Royston, B.C.

Ancaster Nurseries, Ancaster, Ontario

GERMANY

Dietrich Hobbie, Linswege, Oldenburg

HOLLAND

F. J. Grootendurst & Sons, Boskoop

M. Koster & Zonen, Boskoop

J. Blaauw & Co, Boskoop

Vuyk van Nes, Boskoop

Moorheim, Dedemsvaart

JAPAN

K. Wada, PO Box 295, Yokohama

APPENDIX 4

Where to See Rhododendrons

I cannot begin to give a comprehensive list of gardens which have a good selection of rhododendrons, but the following are some of the larger and better known ones, and are, as far as I know, open to the public on at least some days each year. Some of course, such as Wisley, are open virtually all the time.

The best months for visiting them are probably April and May, when the greatest number of species and hybrids is likely to be in flower, but gardens such as Glenarn and Inverewe, with a good range of species and in consequence a great variety of foliage, are fascinating at any time of year. The Scottish Gardens possibly tend to go in more for species, and the English ones for hybrids and mass displays, but of course there are exceptions.

Inverewe, Poolewe, Wester Ross (The National Trust for Scotland)

Crarae, Lochfyneside, Argyll (Sir Ilay Campbell, Bt)

Isle of Gigha, Argyll (Lt-Col Sir James Horlick, Bt)

Strone, Cairndow, Argyll (M. A. C. Noble)

Glenarn, Rhu, Dunbartonshire (A. C. & J. F. A. Gibson)

Brodick Castle, Isle of Arran (The National Trust for Scotland)

Threave, Kirkcudbrightshire (The National Trust for Scotland)

The Royal Botanic Gardens, Inverleith Row, Edinburgh, and its 'annexes' at Benmore, Argyll and Logan, Wigtown

Harlow Car, Harrogate, Yorkshire (The Northern Horticultural Society)

The Savill & Valley Gardens, Windsor Great Park, Berks

Wisley Gardens, Ripley, Woking, Surrey (The Royal Horticultural Society)

Nymans, Handcross, Sussex (The Countess of Rosse)

Leonardslee, Lower Beeding, Sussex (Sir Giles Loder, Bt)

Wakehurst Place, Ardingly, Sussex (Kew Gardens 'annexe')

The Grange, Benenden, Kent (Capt Collingwood Ingram)

Sandling Park, Hythe, Kent (Major A. E. Hardy)

Exbury, near Southampton, Hants (E. de Rothschild)

The Garden House, Buckland Monachorum, Devon

Cotehele, Calstock, Devon

Knighthayes Court, Bolham, Tiverton, Devon

Saltram House, near Plymouth, Devon

Dartington Hall, Dartington, Devon

Killerton, Broad Clyst, Devon

Caerhays Castle, Gorran, St Austell, Cornwall (J. F. Williams)

Lamellan, St Tudy, Bodmin, Cornwall (Major E. W. M. Magor)

Tremeer, St Tudy, Cornwall (Maj-Gen. E. G. W. W. Harrison)

Glendurgan, Mawnan Smith, Cornwall

Trelissick, near Truro, Cornwall

Penjerrick, Budock, Cornwall

Trengwainton, Penzance, Cornwall

Bodnant, Tal-y-Cafn, Colwyn Bay, Denbighshire, N. Wales (Lord Aberconway)

Clyne Castle, Swansea, Wales

Powis Castle, Welshpool, Wales

GARDENS IN AMERICA

University of California Botanic Garden, Berkeley 4, Calif.

Descanso Gardens, 1418 Descanso Dr., La Canada, Calif.

Strybing Arboretum & Botanic Garden, Golden Gate Park, San Francisco, Calif.

Wilmot Memorial Garden, Univ of Florida, Gainsville, Florida (azaleas)

Ida Cason Callaway Gardens, Pine Mountain, Georgia

U.S. National Arboretum, near Montana Ave & Bladenburg Rd N.E., Washington 25, DC

The Arnold Arboretum of Harvard Univ, Jamaica Plain 30, Massachusetts

Beal-Garfield Botanic Gardens, Michigan State Univ, East Lansing, Michigan

Gotelli Arboretum, 66 Crest Dr., South Orange, New Jersey

The Cornell Plantations, Cornell Univ., Ithaca, New Jersey

The New York Botanic Garden, Bronx Park, New York 58

Bayard Cutting Arboretum, Oakdale, Long Island, New York

Planting Fields Arboretum, Planting Fields Rd, Oyster Bay, Long Island, New York

Durand-Eastman Park, on Lake Ontario. c/o Highland Park Herbarium, 5 Castle Park, Rochester 20

The Biltmore Estate, Biltmore Station, Asheville, N. Carolina (a test garden of the American Rhododendron Soc.)

Sarah P. Duke Memorial Garden, Duke Univ., Durham, N. Carolina

Norfolk Botanic Garden, Granby & 35th Sts, Norfolk, Virginia (azaleas)

Eden Park Conservatory, 950 Eden Park Drive, Cincinnati 2, Ohio

Taylor Memorial Arboretum, 10 Ridley Dr., Garden City, Chester, Pa.

Longwood Gardens, Kennett Sq., Pa.

The Morris Arboretum of the Univ. of Penns., Meadowbrook Ave, Philadelphia 18, Pa.

Arthur Hoyt Scott Horticultural Foundation, Swarthmore College, Swarthmore, Pa.

Univ. of Washington Arboretum, Lake Washington Blvd., Seattle 5, Washington.

JAPAN
Donsetsuzan National Park, Hokkaido

Chichibu-Tama National Park, 60 ml N.W. of Tokyo

Fuji-hakone-izu National Park, 50 ml W. of Yokohama

NEW ZEALAND
Botanic Gardens, Christchurch

Pukeiti Rhododendron Trust, New Plymouth

GERMANY
Botanischer Garten und Rhododendron Park, Bremen

Botanischer Garten der Stadt, Dortmund-Brünninghausen

Planten un Blomen, Dammtor, Hamburg (reputed to contain the first rhododendrons planted in continental Europe)

Linswege bei Westerstede, Oldenburg (probably the largest selection of species in Germany)

Munchen-Nymphenburg Botanischer Garten, Munich

Rodenkirchen, near Cologne

BELGIUM
Arboretum de Belder, Kalmthout

HOLLAND
Park Clingendale, The Hague

Experimental Nurseries, Boskoop (contains New Guinea species)

ITALY
Isola Bella, Lake Maggiore

Isola Madra, Lake Maggiore

Giardini Taranto, Lake Maggiore

Tremezzo, Lake Como

AUSTRIA
City Botanic Gardens, Roseggerstrasse 20, Linz

SWEDEN
Botaniska Trädgården, Frölundagatan 22, Göteberg, SV

King Gustav Adolf's Rhododendron Park, Sofiero

Some Useful Addresses

The Royal Horticultural Society, Vincent Sq., London SW1P 2PE.

The Alpine Garden Society, Lye End Link, St John's, Woking, Surrey.

The Scottish Rock Garden Club, 70 High St, Haddington, East Lothian.

The American Rhododendron Society, R.2, Box 105, Sherwood, Oregon 97140.

The New Zealand Rhododendron Association, The Secretary, P.O. Box 28, Palmerston North.

The Australian Rhododendron Society, The Secretary, Olinda, Victoria 3788.

Bibliography

The most comprehensive lists of books and papers that I know of are given in Leach and Bowers.

Allan, Mea. *The Hookers of Kew*, 1967

Barnes, F. Cyril & Forsyth, T. Scott. *Rhododendron in the North*, The Northern Horticultural Society, 1970

Bayley Balfour. 'Observations of Rhododendron Seedlings', *Trans Bot Soc Edin*, 27 (1917) 221–7

Bowers, C. G. *Rhododendrons and Azaleas*, 1960 (2nd edition)

Bridgers, B. T. 'Studies of factors inhibiting the rooting of rhododendron cuttings', *Quar Bull Amer Rhod Soc*, 6 (1952) 186–205 & 207 (1953) 11–28

British Crop Protection Council. *Insecticide and Fungicide Handbook*, (Oxford) 1969

Coats, Alice M. *The Quest for Plants*, 1969

Cowan, J. M. *The Rhododendron Leaf*, 1950

Cowan, J. M. *The Journeys and Plant Introductions of George Forrest, VMH*, 1952

Cox, E. H. M. & P. A. *Modern Rhododendrons*, 1956

Cox, P. A. 'Rhododendron Conservation', *J Roy Hort Soc*, XCVI (1971), 449–55

Cronquist, A. *Evolution and Classification of Flowering Plants*, 1968

Darlington, C. D. & Janaki Anmal, E. K. *Chromosome Atlas of Cultivated Plants*, 1945

Forrest, G. 'Rhododendrons in China', *Gardeners' Chronicle*, LI (1912), 291–2

Forrest, G. 'Notes on the Plants of N. W. Yunnan', *J. Roy Hort Soc*, XL (1915)

George, A. F. 'Modern compact Rhododendron Hybrids', *J Roy Hort Soc*, XCVI (1971), 449–55

Gerard's Herbal, 1597, p. 1221

Hall, I. S. 'An Amateur's Way with Rhododendron Cuttings', *SRGC Journal*, XII (1970), 77–82

Hooker, J. D. *Rhododendrons of the Sikkim Himalaya*, 1848–51

Hortus Kewensis

Hyams, E. *Pleasure from Plants*, 1966

Haworth-Booth, M. *Effective Flowering Shrubs*, 1962

Kingdon-Ward, F. *Rhododendrons*, 1949

Krüssman, Gerd. *Rhododendrons*, 1970

Leach, David G. *Rhododendrons of the World*, 1962

Lee, F. P. *The Azalea Book*, 1958

Lucas Phillips, C. E. 'The Design and Control of Small Gardens', *J Roy Hort Soc*, XCV (1970), 437–44

Merck Index, 8th Edn, 1968 (Rahway, NJ)

Miller, Phillip. *The Gardener's Dictionary*, 8th Edn, 1768

Miller, Phillip & Martyn, Thomas. *The Gardener's and Botanist's Dictionary*, 1807

Parkinson. *Paradisi in Sole*, 1629, p. 424

Regel, Edward von. 'A History of the Rhododendron', *The Garden*, X, 22–9, 1876

Rhododendron Yearbook, 1946–53. RHS

Rhododendron and Camellia Yearbook, 1954–71. RHS

Royal Horticultural Society—*Dictionary of Gardening*

Rhododendron Handbook, The, Part I (1967). RHS

Rhododendron Handbook, The, Part II (1969). RHS

Seithe, Almut. 'Die Haarformen der Gattung Rhododendron L. und die Möglechkeit ihrer taxonomischen Verwertung', *Bot Jb 79*, 3 (1960), 297–393

Simpson, C. M. 'The Propagation of Ericaceae from Cuttings', *SRGC Journal*, XIII (1972), 74–8.

Stevenson *et al. The Species of Rhododendron.* The Rhododendron Society, 1930

Street, F. *Rhododendrons,* 1954

Street, F. *Azaleas,* 1959

Stroyen, H. L. G. '*Masonaphis lambersi* MacGill: an Introduced Aphid Pest of Hybrid Rhododendrons'. *Plant Path* 20 (1971), 196

Thomas, Graham. 'The Artistry of Planting', *J Roy Hort Soc,* XCV (1970), 390–409

Tod, Henry. 'High Calcium or High pH?', *SRGC Journal,* V (1956), 50–5

Tod, Henry. 'Avoiding Trouble with Lime Sensitive Plants', *Gardener's Chronicle/Gardening Illustrated,* Aug 22, 1959, p. 98

Tod, Henry. 'Can Rhododendron Soils be too acid?' *Amateur Gardening,* Jan 16, 1960, 10

Tod, Henry. 'Growth Trials on Sphagnum Compost', *SRGC Journal,* XI (1968), 22–3.

Tod, Henry. 'Nitrogen Sources for Rhododendrons', *Gardener's Chronicle/New Horticulturalist,* March 14, 1969

Tod, Henry. 'Mystery of Tufa and Lime-hating Plants', *Gardener's Chronicle/New Horticulturalist,* Sept 5, 1969, p. 267

Tod, Henry. 'Nitrogen Sources for Mature Rhododendrons', *Gardener's Chronicle/HTJ,* March 5, 1971, p. 33

Tod, Henry. 'Chlorosis in Rhododendrons', Part I, *Gardener's Chronicle/HTJ,* Nov 19, 1971, 17–18. Part II, Dec 3, 1971, 22–5

Wells, J. S. *Plant Propagation Practices,* 1955

Wilson, E. H. & Rehder, A. *A Monograph of Azaleas,* 1921

Acknowledgements

I should like to thank the following:
Dr Norman Robson, for reading the manuscript; Dr Henry Tod, for information on soils; Professor R. D. Lockhart, for information on 'Elizabeth Lockhart' and growing rhododendrons in Aberdeen; Mr Anthony Huxley, for advice; Mr F. Cyril Barnes and the Northern Horticultural Society, for permission to quote findings in *Rhododendron in the North*; Mr C. D. Brickell and his staff at Wisley for allowing me to pick rhododendrons to draw; Mr Stageman and his staff at the Lindley library; the Council of the RHS, for permission to quote from *The Journeys and Plant Introductions of George Forrest, VMH*; Mr E. A. S. la Croix, for taking most of the photographs; Mr R. G. Feldman and Mr P. C. Ower for developing them; Mr P. H. Thomson, for information about squirrels; Mr and Mrs F. J. Greening; Mrs D. E. Bathurst for Latin translation; Mrs D. Carr for German translation and Mrs M. R. Reynolds for typing the classification at the end of the book.

Index

Plants and places listed in the appendices are not referred to here
Page numbers in italic indicate main references
Page numbers in bold indicate illustrations

INDEX